MASTER YOUR EMOTIONS

2 Books in 1: Manage Your Feelings, Overcome Negative Emotions, Analyze People, Manage Overthinking, Stop Anxiety and Depression with Emotional Intelligence

Samantha Scott

© Copyright 2020 by Samantha Scott. All right reserved.

The work contained herein has been produced with the intent to provide relevant knowledge and information on the topic on the topic described in the title for entertainment purposes only. While the author has gone to every extent to furnish up to date and true information, no claims can be made as to its accuracy or validity as the author has made no claims to be an expert on this topic. Notwithstanding, the reader is asked to do their research and consult any subject matter experts they deem necessary to ensure the quality and accuracy of the material presented herein.

This statement is legally binding as deemed by the Committee of Publishers Association and the American Bar Association for the territory of the United States. Other jurisdictions may apply their legal statutes. Any reproduction, transmission, or copying of this material contained in this work without the express written consent of the copyright holder shall be deemed as a copyright violation as per the current legislation in force on the date of publishing and the subsequent time thereafter. All additional works derived from this material may be claimed by the holder of this copyright.

The data, depictions, events, descriptions, and all other information forthwith are considered to be true, fair, and accurate unless the work is expressly described as a work of fiction. Regardless of the nature of this work, the Publisher is exempt from any responsibility of actions taken by the reader in conjunction with this work. The Publisher acknowledges that the reader acts of their own accord and releases the author and Publisher of any responsibility for the observance of tips, advice, counsel, strategies, and techniques that may be offered in this volume.

TABLE OF CONTENTS

EMOTIONAL INTELLIGENCE
Ultimate Guide to Mastering Your Feelings, Increase Self-Confidence and Self-Discipline, Overcome Anxiety and Win at Life

Introduction 3
Chapter 1 *What Is Emotional Intelligence?* 4
Chapter 2 *The Benefits Of Emotional Intelligence* 8
Chapter 3 *Communication Styles* 12
Chapter 4 *Emotional Intelligence In The Workplace* 23
Chapter 5 *Emotional Intelligence In Your Relationships* 27
Chapter 6 *Increasing Your Level Of Emotional Intelligence Part 1-Motivation* 32
Chapter 7 *Increasing Your Level Of Emotional Intelligence Part 2- Your Emotions And Needs* 42
Chapter 8 *Increasing Your Level Of Emotional Intelligence Part 3- Empathy* 48
Chapter 9 *Increasing Your Level Of Emotional Intelligence Part 4- Self-Regulation* 56
Chapter 10 *Increasing Your Level Of Emotional Intelligence Part 5- Self-Awareness* 65
Conclusion 70
Description 71

HOW TO ANALYZE PEOPLE
Read Human Behaviors, Learn Body Language, And Analyze Nonverbal Communication Using Emotional Intelligence

Introduction 75
Chapter 1 *The Purpose Of Analyzing Others* 78
Chapter 2 *Can You Really Understand The Mind By Watching The Body?* 81
Chapter 3 *The Uses Of Analyzing Others* 85
Chapter 4 *Looking At Nonverbal Cues* 90
Chapter 5 *Understanding The Movements Of The Face* 96
Chapter 6 *Understanding The Movements Of The Body* 104
Chapter 7 *Understanding The Movements Of The Legs And Feet* 110
Chapter 8 *Proxemics* 116
Chapter 9 *Haptics* 121

Chapter 10 *Identifying Body Language Clusters* 124
Chapter 11 *Using Body Language* 133
Conclusion 139
Description 141

EMOTIONAL INTELLIGENCE

Ultimate Guide to Mastering Your Feelings, Increase Self-Confidence and Self-Discipline, Overcome Anxiety and Win at Life

Samantha Scott

© Copyright 2020 by Samantha Scott. All right reserved.

The work contained herein has been produced with the intent to provide relevant knowledge and information on the topic on the topic described in the title for entertainment purposes only. While the author has gone to every extent to furnish up to date and true information, no claims can be made as to its accuracy or validity as the author has made no claims to be an expert on this topic. Notwithstanding, the reader is asked to do their research and consult any subject matter experts they deem necessary to ensure the quality and accuracy of the material presented herein.

This statement is legally binding as deemed by the Committee of Publishers Association and the American Bar Association for the territory of the United States. Other jurisdictions may apply their legal statutes. Any reproduction, transmission, or copying of this material contained in this work without the express written consent of the copyright holder shall be deemed as a copyright violation as per the current legislation in force on the date of publishing and the subsequent time thereafter. All additional works derived from this material may be claimed by the holder of this copyright.

The data, depictions, events, descriptions, and all other information forthwith are considered to be true, fair, and accurate unless the work is expressly described as a work of fiction. Regardless of the nature of this work, the Publisher is exempt from any responsibility of actions taken by the reader in conjunction with this work. The Publisher acknowledges that the reader acts of their own accord and releases the author and Publisher of any responsibility for the observance of tips, advice, counsel, strategies, and techniques that may be offered in this volume.

INTRODUCTION

If you have purchased this book, you are likely someone that wants a significant change in their life. Seeking change is entirely normal in a person's life. These feelings often come about when a person realizes there are some flaws in their life and how they relate to others.

Increasing your level of emotional intelligence will lead to a variety of positive changes in life. Increased emotional intelligence is especially important if you are someone that is looking to bring more success into their work experience as well as their personal life.

A person's idea of success varies wildly from one person to another. Some people may feel that workplace success and wealth are the definitions of success, whereas others may feel that developing strong relationships is a success. Whichever your perspective, increasing your emotional intelligence will lead to improvements in both of these areas of your life, including many more.

Due to our society's nature, many people operate on an "auto-pilot" mode throughout their day, never stopping to think about their lives or actions. By reading this book, you take a step back and evaluate yourself, which is the first step to making change. This book will teach you how to live a healthier and more fulfilling life without ever having to think too much about it.

It is not easy to change your life, especially if you have been living a certain way for a long time. After reading this book, I hope that you are well-equipped to begin making changes in your life, no matter how small. You have already taken the first step by choosing this book; all that is left is to begin taking action. You are going to learn a lot of information here, so prepare yourself.

The key here will be practice, as improving emotional intelligence does not happen overnight. It is proven to improve with some practice, and you will need to stick with it to see lasting changes. Remember, everyone's perception of reality is different. You can start small by asking others for their opinion and try to understand what they are feeling, while also getting in touch with and communicating your feelings.

Throughout this book, we will look at what emotional intelligence is and how you can improve your emotional intelligence. This book is chock full of information that will prove useful to you in your pursuit of the life you have dreamt of! Make sure you share this book with friends and family so they too, can gain the knowledge to improve their emotional intelligence.

CHAPTER 1
What Is Emotional Intelligence?

In this chapter, we will begin the book by examining what emotional intelligence consists of and how it can be useful to you. This chapter will give you a great foundation on which to build throughout this book. Without further ado, we are going to define Emotional Intelligence.

What Is Emotional Intelligence (EI)?

Emotional intelligence is a term that was developed by two researchers, Peter Salavoy and John Mayer, in the field of psychology. We define emotional intelligence as a person's ability to recognize, understand, and control their emotions. Sometimes, we also describe it as a person's ability to identify, understand, and influence other people's feelings. In the simplest terms, EI is the ability to be aware that emotions drive human behaviors and have the power to impact other people. By learning how to manage your feelings, you will be able to affect yourself and others positively.

The following components make up emotional intelligence:

- **Self-awareness:**

Self-awareness allows people to understand their strengths and weaknesses. Understanding them gives the person a better understanding of how to react properly to other people and certain situations. When a person reflects on their emotions, they begin to gain self-awareness. To grow emotional intelligence, a person will need to think about their feelings and how they most often react in negative situations. When a person becomes more aware of which emotions they are dealing with, they can begin to manage and control them appropriately, leading to a higher self-awareness level.

- **Self-regulation:**

When a person has self-regulation, high EI comes into play by allowing the person to properly regulate their emotions to keep it in check when needed.

- **Motivation:**

People that have high emotional intelligence tend to have more motivation, which makes them more optimistic. Having more optimism causes them to have more resilience towards negativity.

- **Empathy:**

Usually, people who are more successful in connecting with others exhibit strong traits of empathy and compassion.

- **Social skills:**

Likely, a person with high emotional intelligence has the social skills needed to showcase their respect and care for others. For this reason, those who have higher EI tend to get along better with people in general.

Attributes of People With Low Emotional Intelligence

A high level of emotional intelligence is well sought after in work environments and general life because a person's emotional intelligence level plays a significant role in interacting with other people. People who struggle with low emotional intelligence, such as family, friends, employers, and co-workers, make many social situations tense and difficult. In most cases, it could be your emotional intelligence that needs some work.

To help you understand further and identify whether or not you have low emotional intelligence, here are nine common indicators:

1. Getting into frequent arguments.

Everyone probably knows at least one person in their life that always seems to be arguing with other people. People in your life, such as friends, family, or sometimes even strangers, will end up arguing with these types of people. The reason behind this is because individuals who have low EI struggle to understand what other people's emotions are and argue with them without considering how the other person may be feeling.

2. Inability to understand the feelings of others.

Individuals with low EI tend to be very oblivious regarding other people's emotions and feelings. For instance, they have a hard time understanding why their friends might be upset with them or why their co-workers are annoyed. In addition to that, they often feel like they should be annoyed at other people because of other people's expectations of them to understand their feelings. While this holds for high EI people, people with low EI can't properly assess other people's feelings. The mere topic of emotions tends to cause people with low EI to feel very exasperated.

3. Think that everyone else is too sensitive.

Those who have low emotional intelligence may tend to tell jokes at inappropriate moments. For example, they may make a joke right after a funeral or a tragic event. When people don't react the way they expect to their mistime jokes, the person with low EI may feel that other people are acting too sensitive. They struggle to understand others' feelings and therefore have trouble sensing the emotional tone during certain situations.

4. Refuse to listen to other people's perspectives.

People with low Emotional Intelligence tend to feel that they are always right and will intensely defend their stance and refuse to hear what other people may have to say. These people tend to be pessimists and are very critical of other people's feelings.

5. Blame others when things go wrong.

People with low emotional intelligence don't understand their feelings and how they tend to lead to problems. When things aren't going their way, their initial reaction is to blame others around them. They often will blame the essence of the situation or other people's behaviors. A common rebuttal that these individuals use is that they had no other choice for what they did and that other people do not understand their circumstances. They tend to feel victimized to avoid responsibility.

6. Unable to handle emotionally fueled situations.

When a situation arises where strong emotions also arise, people with low EI struggle to comprehend them. They tend to try to flee from these situations to avoid having to deal with confrontations. It is also extremely common for these individuals to hide their emotions and feelings from others.

7. Sudden Emotional Explosions.

As we will see in the section regarding examples of high emotional intelligence, one of the main points is a person's ability to maintain and regulate emotions. Individuals who struggle with emotional intelligence have a hard time understanding their emotions and then regulating them. They often have emotional outbursts that are unexpected and appear to be uncontrollable.

8. Maintaining friendships is difficult.

The people with low EI often come off as insensitive and abrasive, which creates difficulty for them when creating friendships and bonding with other people. Since friendship requires to give and take from both people, those with low EI struggle with friendships. They also have a hard time with other friendship components, where the sharing of emotions, emotional support, and compassion are required.

9. Lack of empathy.

Since individuals with low EI have trouble understanding other people's emotions, they can often feel empathy for others. They simply do not understand what emotions the other person is feeling, making it very hard for them to see things from their perspective, let alone empathize.

Attributes of People With High Emotional Intelligence

Since personalities are very different from person to person, how a person develops their emotional intelligence depends on the individual. Here are some common examples of attributes that people with high emotional intelligence tend to possess:

1. They can express themselves respectfully and openly without fearing that they will offend other people.
2. They often show resilience in the face of new initiatives, even if they don't agree with them.

3. They are always flexible, even if it is not convenient for them.
4. They like to spend time with their coworkers outside of working hours.
5. There is the freedom to be creative, and they celebrate this.
6. They often listen actively during meetings and contribute when they have something to say.
7. They always listen to other people's problems and show compassion to them. They are very kind and caring individuals.

One of the most important things that high emotional intelligence helps with is leadership. Leaders who have good emotional intelligence can build a team of more deeply connected people and be involved in a single vision. They often care more about the work that they do rather than just producing for the sake of getting things done. A leader with high EI can motivate and empower employees and is also good at navigating through complex and difficult decisions while showing an excellent emotional response.

High emotional intelligence does not mean that someone is always happy or in a positive mood. It simply means that the person can make good decisions regarding their actions when faced with a difficult situation. They can process their emotions to make decisions that aren't fueled by their feelings.

In the chapters that follow, we will look at how you can improve your emotional intelligence level and the benefits that this will bring you.

CHAPTER 2
The Benefits Of Emotional Intelligence

Now that you understand what emotional intelligence is, we will begin talking about how it can benefit you. There are numerous benefits to having a high level of emotional intelligence. In this chapter, we will look at them in detail to better understand the importance of the information contained within this book.

How Can Emotional Intelligence Benefit You?

One of the most important skills to learn in life is emotional intelligence. Emotional intelligence will benefit you for several reasons; most of these reasons stem from the ability to read and understand others' behavior. In this section, we are going to look at these benefits.
- It will help you to read people.

It is important to understand how to read people at the most basic human connection level and understand their motivations. Reading people will help you in knowing how to approach people and connect to them. We will look at an example of this to help you better understand the importance of emotional intelligence. If you are looking to get directions from a stranger on the street, you will need to read all of the people around you to determine who will be the most approachable person to ask. To do this, you will need to take stock of several things about each person you see, including their body language and their overall energy, to find someone that appears more friendly so you can ask them for directions. You would want to be able to read the body language of someone who looks unhappy or angry, as that is a person you may not want to approach in the middle of the street.
- It will help you to read and understand social encounters.

By increasing your emotional intelligence level and learning to read people better, you can advance your life in many ways. For instance, if you seek promotion from your boss, you may be able to read their body language, verbal and non-verbal messages, and their overall mood to determine if it's the right time to ask for a promotion or a raise.
You can determine what more your boss wants to see from you to improve your performance or gain a promotion at a lower level.
- It will help you with dating and relationships.

The above is also true for other types of relationships, such as a romantic relationship. If there is someone you're romantically interested in, analyzing them properly will allow you to understand what your relationship with them is like in their eyes. By assessing your relationship's level and strength, you may be better able to ask them out on a date or to initiate more conversations with them.

- It will help you to communicate better.

Increasing your level of emotional intelligence will give you the knowledge you will need to tailor your communication style to fit the exchange type. Communicating with more skill allows you to grow closer with people and to build more rapport.

For instance, you wouldn't talk to your significant other in the way that you would talk to your boss. Learning to tailor your communication and entire demeanor to match the situation and the relationship is crucial for finding the right response to someone. If you notice that your boss looks unhappy, stressed, and angry that day by assessing his facial expression and posture, you may not want to approach him with a 3-week vacation request that day. Most people who can read the situation would choose another day where their boss is better at asking for a favor. This book will teach you the tools and skills needed to assess anyone you want so you can find the right moments to ask for what you need and to further your desired relationships.

- It will help you to read people's personalities.

Emotional intelligence will help you in your social interactions and relationships by giving you the ability to understand the different personality types that humans may exhibit. By gaining the ability to read and understand different personality types, you will be able to better connect with people in your life.

You have surely heard and used the term *personality* before, but we will begin by ensuring our definitions of the word *personality* are the same before we move on. The definition of the term personality and what it means varies greatly depending on who you ask. Still, in general, personality is a way of describing one's potential behaviors and actions in any given situation. For this reason, determining someone's personality and even your own can give you insight into how and why you or another person may act. In a way, it is a description of your character as it examines and explains your thoughts, behaviors, and feelings.

Understanding personality types is one of the most important benefits of increasing your level of emotional intelligence. Understanding this allows you to account for natural differences in the way people act or display behavior simply because of what type of person they are. These personality types create different types of people who may act slightly differently in different situations. Knowing what to look for to understand someone's personality type will aid in further analyzing their actions. Knowing what to look for will also allow you to anticipate how they may act in different situations or respond to things you may want to say. It is an invaluable tool in the analysis for understanding someone's current actions and potential future reactions.

There are four different categories we look at when determining personality types. Each category has two different options to choose from. People will tend to fit into one of the two options. These four categories come together in a unique combination for the person to create many different personality types. We will examine each of the four categories in depth before learning how they come together to create personality types.

The first category included in personality assessment is introvert and extrovert, the second is sensing and intuition; next is thinking and feeling, and finally, judging and perceiving. We give each of these traits a letter representing it for ease of giving each of the different combinations a name. As you can imagine, the letters for each trait are as follows; introvert (I), extrovert (E), sensing (S), intuition (N), thinking (T), feeling (F), judging (J), and finally, perceiving (P). You may see the different personality types referred to by their corresponding letters in the future, but you can simply reference this section as a guide.

There are debates in the world of psychology about which plays more of a role in developing a person and their personality, the traits they were born with, or the traits they gained through their environment in infancy and childhood. This debate dates back some time, and many people have very strong stances on this topic.

Do we have the personality that we were born with, and is it fixed? Or do we develop into the people we become because of how, where, and who raised us?

The side of this debate that you stand on may influence your view of personality and its origins. While we may never definitively know the answer, having a high level of emotional intelligence will allow you to accurately perceive people's emotions and personality traits, regardless of whether they were born with them or acquired them over time.

We will look at a real-world example that will show you how this skill will benefit you in your own life. Let's say you know a person's entire family, and they are all of the extrovert variety. If you are of the mindset that we are a product of our environment, you would think without a doubt, even before you meet this person, that they must be an extrovert because their family consisted of extroverts. If you are of the mindset that we are born with our personality, and our environment does not change this, you may approach the first meeting with this person, thinking that there is a 50/50 chance that they are one or the other. Take note of your stance as this may lead you to enter an analysis situation with preconceived ideas about a person and their personality.

Another way that personality can play into your analysis of people is that we all enter the world each day with an idea of how we wish to be perceived. Keeping this in mind can make analyzing a person more difficult than showing their true personality in each interaction. There is a lot of work to be done on emotional intelligence to ensure that you are reading a person correctly. Luckily, growing up in a world full of people, we have years of practice and informal research to help us. Since we all put forth some kind of image each time that we enter the world, we can understand that everyone around us is putting their best foot forward when they go out into the world. Knowing and understanding the most common ways people portray themselves in the world can help us understand the true person beneath them. We will examine some of the most common types of facades that you will encounter daily.

The Areas of Your Life That Emotional Intelligence Will Positively Impact

There are numerous benefits to learning how to increase your emotional intelligence level, including the benefits we looked at in the previous section. This section will look at the different areas of your life that this skill will help.

- In the workplace

For example, imagine you want to read and understand a potential client in the workplace to strategize your pitch to them if you are a salesperson. You would easily be able to navigate your approach.

- In your relationships
- In social settings and situations

Maybe you want to start building more meaningful connections with people, so you want to find the right type of people to build friendships and relationships with. It is also important to be able to read people you already have relationships with. If a friend looks unhappy, you may want to have a conversation about why they are feeling down.

- In your family life

As you can see above, increasing your emotional intelligence level will benefit every area of your life. Regardless of your reasoning for increasing your level of emotional intelligence, the scenarios above all have one thing in common; You need to understand the basics when it comes to the nature of humans, their emotions, and their actions if you are going to be successful in these types of situations. Understanding people and reading unspoken messages can help you be a better friend, significant other, or co-worker. By reading this book and increasing your level of emotional intelligence, you will improve your relationships and your life as a whole.

CHAPTER 3
Communication Styles

In this chapter, we are going to look at the importance that communication plays in emotional intelligence. As you know, communication is essential to connecting with other humans, so it is so important to read and understand others. We will look at the relationship between communication and emotional intelligence before moving onto the most effective communication styles exhibited by those with a high emotional intelligence level.

The Relationship Between Communication and Emotional Intelligence

This section will look at communication and how it can help you develop, improve, and maintain healthy and strong relationships through emotional intelligence. We will do this by learning to understand and read the communication methods of others. Communication is a very large component of relationships and ensuring that they are healthy and long-lasting.

As you know by now, some people are born with a strong natural ability to analyze others because they received the gift of a high level of emotional intelligence at birth. To review, we will revisit the importance of emotional intelligence. Emotional intelligence allows you to understand other people's emotions and take a look at things from their perspective, as well as being able to understand your own emotions. As I mentioned in the previous chapter, two important skills, analyzing people and emotional intelligence, are closely related. Both of these skills require a deep understanding of human communication.

Communication is not only an important part of relationships but also day to day life in general. Before you have a relationship with another person, you will likely communicate with them in some form, even if you see them only once. For example, when you go to the gas station to fill up your car, you may pull in to see that there is a line-up of cars all waiting for their turn at the pump. You may give the nod or a look to someone else in their car to communicate for them to "go ahead" or "wait." Communication is essential to living in a society of humans and has been around long before the modern languages we know and use now. Communication does not have to be verbal; it can come in different forms that don't involve speaking. We will look at these different forms a little later in this chapter. Communicating with skill will help you in your workplace, in your home and family, in your leisure activities, and in your everyday interactions with other people.

Reading and analyzing a person effectively allows you to tailor your communication style to one that fits the other person's so that you can better understand each other. Reading and analyzing a person effectively also allows you to grow closer with people and build more rapport. This kind of effective communication encompasses both nonverbal and verbal forms of communication. We will look at effective communication later on in this chapter.

Nonverbal Communication Versus Verbal Communication

Nonverbal communication contributes mainly to the formation of first impressions in humans. Because of this, it is very important to understand what the things we see are telling us. We can learn a lot about a person before speaking a word to them by simply examining their nonverbal actions. We do this already in our day to day life simply because we are visual creatures. Our eyes perceive the world around us, and this is no different when perceiving people. Because of this, everyone, including you, already has a foundation to begin reading nonverbal communication in a more focused and specific way. Learning what to look for and deciphering this type of communication involves fine-tuning a skill that we already possess.

Communication runs deeper than just the words you say to people. The way you hold yourself, tone of voice, and your facial expressions say much more about your message than the actual message itself. For instance, if you ask your significant other to help you with the dishes while having a frown on your face with your arms crossed, it will make the question sound a lot more aggressive. If you asked that question with a smile on your face and a relaxed body posture, your significant other might be more likely to oblige to your request. Do you see the importance of HOW you deliver a message versus WHAT your message is? Expert communicators will be able to deliver negative messages but still have it be received well. Expert communication skills are a highly sought-after skill in the professional world as to how you deliver an extremely important message in executives, customers, and colleagues' eyes.

How to Communicate Effectively

Effective communication uses a process that uses the following structure;
- Observations

Your observations of the situation, yourself, or the other person, stated factually, begin nonviolent communication. You must observe without feelings and judgments involved and simply the facts of the matter.
- Feelings

The next step is to express your feelings and allow the other person to express theirs, which you must do without judgment and blame. In this case, you have to do this in the absence of judgment for yourself as well. You must also avoid assuming anything at this stage.

- Needs

Now, you must do a little bit of work to recognize your personal needs that are going unmet, which caused you to feel the way you previously stated. You can also state what your needs are going forward.

- Requests

After all of the above, you can then offer a solution to the problem or a request that you have involving this situation or possible situations of this sort that may arise in the future.

By communicating effectively, the other person feels heard and understood, and this prevents them from becoming defensive, which would lead them to react and respond defensively. This type of communication allows both people to feel heard and understood, and it reaches a solution or an understanding in a much shorter period.

Differences In Communication Styles Between Those With High EI and Low EI

If someone has the skill of "good communication," what does this mean? Good communication skills mean that they can communicate (both giving and receiving information) effectively and accurately. This communication involves things you are feeling, things you see, and more abstract things like concepts and ideas. This concept goes hand in hand with emotional intelligence.

When it comes to communication in all different types of relationships, emotional intelligence is something that everybody needs to know and learn. In this section, we are going to look at the ways that people with high EI communicate.

The Importance of Listening

Listening is an essential part of communication that many people forget. Listening is just as much a part of communication as speaking is, and one of the keys to successful communication in relationships is listening well. Listening well is a skill that must be practiced and maintained, which will greatly help you increase your emotional intelligence level.

Half of the skill of communicating involves the ability to receive and interpret the communications of others. We will look at some of the things that make a good listener that will help you to become a skillful nonviolent communicator. Listening includes what we observe with our eyes just as much as what we hear. Now that you understand both verbal and nonverbal communication, we will look deeper into both of these to understand how to be the best communicator possible.

The first thing that makes a good listener is being able to listen actively. *Active listening* can make you an effective listener and, therefore, an effective all-around communicator. Active listening involves hearing what the person is saying to you and taking it in and trying to understand it. It involves a deeper concentration than just hearing and involves understanding what people tell you as a whole rather than just the words themselves. We will often hear the person speaking to us, but we will not be paying attention to what they are saying. Paying close attention helps us understand the information that the person is sharing with us and then respond accordingly and thoughtfully. This type of listening will help you get the most out of your communications no matter who they are with and will make your transition to Emotional intelligence much smoother.

The second thing to note when becoming a better listener is your intention. Many times, we will listen with the intent to respond. Instead of paying close attention to the person that we are speaking to and listening to what they tell us, we listen for the end of their turn to say what we want to say. We may also be thinking of what we want to say next for the entire duration that the other person is speaking. Instead, we want to listen with the intent to understand. Listening requires an open mind. If our mind is full of thoughts about how we will respond and what we will say next, we cannot listen and process what we hear. If we can actively listen with the intent to hear and understand, rather than play our part in the conversation, we can develop a greater understanding of other people. We can also increase our understanding of what they are saying to us to decide then how we want to contribute to the conversation and the best way to do so. Communicating this way comes into play with emotional intelligence because understanding the person we speak to will help us understand their needs and feelings. Understanding needs and feelings will make us better able to contribute to their well-being, which is very important in emotional intelligence.

Another thing that makes a good listener is the ability to communicate while listening. In saying this, it does not mean that you are talking over the other person or nodding furiously throughout the conversation. Listening well involves gently and subtly telling the person you are hearing them and paying attention to what they tell you. There will be appropriate moments in a conversation where you can tell the person you understand them, hear them, and listen to them. You can do this by saying, "oh yes," "Oh my!" or "mhmm." Doing this will make the person feel heard and, in turn, they will be more inclined to continue sharing their words with you—the second part of communicating while listening is being able to ask questions. Sometimes you will want to ask questions, especially if you have been listening actively and understanding the person. If you need clarification or would like the person to explain something further, it is acceptable to clarify a specific point or concept. You must only ask at the appropriate moments. The other person will likely welcome the active listening you are doing (that involves asking questions), the commitment to understanding, and the interest you are showing in what they are saying.

To take this communication while listening even further, you must also decide whether your input is necessary at each point in the conversation. Sometimes we enjoy hearing ourselves speak our own opinions, and we cannot wait to speak to them! However, we are already well aware of our own opinions, and we don't need to hear them again if necessary. Before contributing to a conversation, briefly determine the intention behind your input. If the intention is to genuinely contribute, then go ahead and do so at the appropriate moment. However, if the intention is to showcase your knowledge or prove your opinion, it may not be necessary to contribute, and you may be better off just listening. If you are practicing active listening, the response you decide to give may change drastically from what you would otherwise have said if you had been listening with the intent to respond. The reason for this is because you have understood the person's words before then, forming a thoughtful response. That is if you even deem a response necessary. Sometimes communication is about listening and not speaking at all. We may decide after listening to a person intently that we do not need to respond at all.

This concept is important for emotional intelligence as the intent of our contribution to a conversation is very different if we are using violent or emotional intelligence. For example, in violent communication, our input intends to showcase our knowledge of a certain topic to make the person feel bad. On the other hand, if we are practicing emotional intelligence, we may decide that our input is not necessary as it would only be to make the person feel bad, and we may decide just to listen instead. This type of listening and determining intent is what makes the difference between these two types of communication, as noticing your intent in the first place is necessary to make any sort of change.

Blaming Versus Understanding

Effective communication *does not* involve anger, blaming the other person, trying to guilt them, blaming, shaming, or judging them.

Communicating in this way has negative impacts on the people with whom we are communicating. As this is violent communication, it causes internal harm. If we are speaking in this way, we may cause harm to ourselves. If we communicate in this way with others, we can cause internal harm to others. In time, this type of communication can lead to anger and resentment, and if we speak to ourselves in this way, it can eventually lead to depression.

Often, we don't even know we are using violent communication, as it may be quite a standard way of interacting. Many societies model violent communication, and thus, the people who grow up in them don't realize that there is any other way to communicate. This upbringing causes many interactions to be full of anger and hate and involve raised voices and harsh words. Sometimes, this leads to physical violence.

Aggressive communication aims to lower a person's feelings of self-worth, ignores their needs, and is void of compassion. It can happen on both the part of the speaker and the listener. Below are some examples of different forms of violent communication for your reference.

1. **Moral Judgement or Evaluation**

"Jennifer is lazy."

In this example, the speaker is using judgment. They are also labeling Jennifer and being critical of her. They are evaluating her and doing so in a judgemental way. In this type of violent communication, the speaker often sees the other person as being wrong.

2. **Denying Responsibility**

"It's not my fault; the policy states that I have to fire you."

In this example of violent communication, the speaker refuses to take responsibility for their actions and blame them on policies, regulations, and rules. In this example, the person may also blame their thoughts or feelings on other people, rules, social norms, or anything other than their decision-making.

3. **Demanding**

"You need to do my homework for me."

In this example, the speaker implies (or sometimes explicitly states) that there is the threat of punishment, of having to take the blame, or of losing a reward if they do not comply with the demand. We also see this type of reverse, where a reward comes if the person complies with the demand. This example is a manipulative form of communication, which is also a type of demand.

4. **Lack of Compassion**

"Were you sick yesterday, or did you just not feel like showing up?"

In this type of example, *lacking compassion,* there are numerous ways to show up in an interaction. At its core, this type of violent communication involves the speaker intentionally sounding like they are trying to fix a situation but doing so in a way that involves correcting the listener, shutting them down, trying to educate them, one-upping them, or interrogating them. In this way, the speaker does not show compassion but is trying to be the voice of reason where the other person did not solicit it.

While the person who is ineffectively communicating may not realize it, it can result in the listener following whatever the request is out of feelings of obligation, fear of punishment, shame, fear, or guilt. Thus, this type of communication can be quite manipulative and controlling, as it forces others' actions.

You may get what you want out of creating this type of situation, but the negative ways it can impact your relationships and mental health are worth mentioning. Firstly, if you speak to others in this way, the chances you speak to yourself are quite high. By not being compassionate or empathetic to others, you are likely unaware of how to be compassionate or empathetic to yourself. If this is true, it means that your mental health and your emotional well-being will suffer. By learning how to use compassion and empathy toward others, you will learn how to use it in your intrapersonal interactions. Secondly, by speaking violently toward others, it can cause your relationships to suffer. If you speak to your family members, such as your children, in this way, to get them to do what you want, they will more than likely develop feelings of resentment toward you. If this occurs, it becomes a discussion of whether it is worth it to you to have others' actions controlled by your words, or if you would rather have strong and genuine relationships that don't involve fear, shame, and guilt.

On the other hand, effectively communicating doesn't involve any of the above. Instead, it involves reaching a mutual understanding between you and the person with whom you are communicating. Effective communication is often called *compassionate communication*. This type of communication is the exact opposite of the type of communication that we just finished discussing above, and instead of blaming, it involves understanding.

How to Communicate Based on Your Analysis of People

Different people will respond in different ways to different styles of communication. For example, for someone introverted, who tends to observe and spend a lot of time thinking, you would communicate with them in a specific way.

To do this, you could play into their thinking and judging traits by explaining facts and statistics to them, laying out the pros and cons for them, and explaining why something is a practical option. We would ensure to explain this in a non-threatening and gentle way as this person is introverted. This type of person would respond well to this communication style because they would tend to spend time solitarily thinking out facts and planning their life well in advance. You may also have someone you need to communicate with less cut and dry in terms of being on one extreme of the personality type spectrum. Let's say we encounter an introverted person, sensing, feeling, perceiving an individual. This individual is similar to our last example in that they are both introverts, but the way they make decisions and handle their emotions is vastly different. Knowing the difference is crucial in communicating most effectively with each of these people. This individual is quite in touch with their emotions; they let their feelings and emotions guide them, and they are more comfortable keeping their options open and seeing where life takes them than planning far in advance. This person would benefit from a different type of communication style. While you would still want to approach them in a non-threatening and gentle manner, you would want to emphasize in a conversation how something may make them feel and the many options/outcomes that are possible. This communication style can help in a situation where you want them to see your point of view, or you would like to guide them in a future endeavor. Because there are so many different combinations of personality types, it may seem like an impossible task to remember them all. However, the reality is that if you simply understand and remember the four main categories, you will be well-equipped to enter the world with enough insight to engage anybody in a way most fitting for them.

How we communicate and listen with different types of people can be very different depending on our relationship with them. How we demonstrate, listening behavior is very different if we listen to our boss to speak than if we are listening to our friend. While it is important to show our friends and family that we are listening to them, we can do so with much less formality of body language. In a one on one meeting with a boss or a superior of some sort, it is important to show them respectful body language. We demonstrate to them that we are listening with eye contact and a few silent nods throughout the conversation. We avoid interruption and asking too many questions until the person finishes speaking. We maintain good posture and sit relatively still to avoid making unnecessary distractions. We ensure not to gaze off for too long to avoid seeming uninterested and unprofessional. When it comes to listening to a friend or a peer, the body language of listening is much less formal. While we do not want to show that we are bored or ignoring them, we can sit or stand with a much less rigid posture. Leaning or slouching a little is acceptable and even welcomed to demonstrate a relaxed attitude. If we were to be too rigid and quiet, we might end up making them feel uncomfortable. We can laugh and agree verbally, and even ask questions at the appropriate time to show them that we are interested and engaged. This type of active participation in the conversation while listening demonstrates care and concern for the subject matter and the person delivering it. It is more important in a professional setting to demonstrate respect for the subject matter and the person delivering it.

There may also be differences in how we demonstrate listening, depending on the person we are listening to. If we are listening to a person younger than us, it is appropriate to act and listen in a familiar way- such as that stated previously, as a peer or a friend. If we communicate with our elders by a significant margin of time, it may be necessary to conduct ourselves more professionally. Communicating with them also includes listening to them professionally, even if they are our friends or family members. People who are older than us by a large enough amount of time may enjoy teaching us things or telling us stories to impart knowledge to us. In this case, it is appropriate to listen and engage but not interrupt with belly laughter or questions until the end of the story or the lesson. Doing this shows respect for their experience and knowledge.

When speaking over the phone, it is very important to be able to listen well, but it becomes more complicated because there is no body language to read or to demonstrate, for that matter. We do not want to continuously interrupt the person by telling them that we are listening, but we also do not want to have extended periods of radio silence to wonder if we have hung up the phone. The key is balance. We must show that we are listening by finding appropriate moments- during a pause or a quiet moment to agree or to say a brief 'yes' or 'mhm.' Too many statements of agreement and the person will not be able to finish what they are saying. While body language is absent for the person to see with their eyes, there are still voice tones and volumes to pick up on. Because we cannot read the other person's face, we want to ensure we are doing whatever we can to start the conversation on a good note by sounding engaged. For example, if you are taking part in a phone interview or a work-related phone call, you need to ensure that you pay attention to the following points. To sound clear and attentive, it helps to have proper body language even if you are sitting alone in a room of your home. Instead of sitting on your couch in pajamas, sit at a desk or chair with a table in front. Put on some type of professional attire. Sit with your feet planted on the floor and your shoulders back. Take note of your facial expression throughout your conversation, because people can hear the shape of your mouth in your voice through the phone. Imagine this person is sitting across the table from you. Accounting for all of these points will come through in your voice dynamics and will show the other person that you are prepared and serious about the interaction even though it is over the phone.

Communication Styles

Before closing this chapter, we will do a self-examination to determine what type of communicator we are most often. Communication comes in many different forms, but we will look at different verbal communication styles in this case. We may all exhibit a combination of all of these styles but can usually pin ourselves down to one style most of the time. Understanding this about ourselves will aid us in communicating our thoughts and ideas more effectively. Still, it will also help us better receive and understand the communication of others' thoughts and ideas. There are four styles of verbal communication that we will examine. They are as follows:

The first communication style we will explore is the Aggressive Communication Style. This communication style comes out of a place of fear. This person fears they will not be heard or understood, and therefore they enter into interaction or conversation with a loud volume and an attitude of entitlement. They approach the conversation with a wide stance and an aggressive posture. They feel the need to shout over others and force their point of view. This communication style can often have the exact effect the communicator is trying to avoid. People may not listen to the content of the sentences because they are distracted by the way the person conveyed their thoughts. When people come face to face with an aggressive communication style, they tend to become defensive and closed-off, unwilling to engage much further in the interaction.

The second is the Passive/Submissive Communication Style. This type of communicator prefers to avoid conflict at all costs. They would rather please people than to make their opinion known. They can be swayed easily and speak with a very low volume. They attempt to shrink themselves down using their body language with hunched shoulders and crossed arms. They feel that their opinions are not valid and apologetic if they feel that someone disagrees. Other people will approach this type of communicator in an exasperated manner as they feel that they have to walk on eggshells to preserve their feelings.

The next is the Passive-Aggressive Communication Style. These communicators initially show one type of attitude on the outside, that their words do not match. They use passive, self-shrinking body language, therefore, appearing to be passive and non-confrontational on the outside, while aggressively communicating with their words. It is the combination of both of the previous two styles of communication. They tend to speak aggressively to indirectly make a point but act out passively in front of the person. Their words are aggressive, but they deliver them in a passive style. They will use a low volume and a gentle tone while saying something likely to cause confrontation or make someone angry. People tend to become frustrated when dealing with this type of communicator because they have to pay close attention to figure out what they are trying to say. People who wish to be of an aggressive style but are afraid to do so often use this communication style.

The final verbal communication style is the Assertive Communication Style. This style of communication is rooted in confidence and self-assuredness. People who communicate in this way have confident body language and maintain eye contact. They are relaxed but engaged. They are emphatic but maintain an average volume and tone of voice. They are secure in their stance both literally and figuratively and are unafraid of rejection or a disagreeing party. They communicate their points with a calm but firm demeanor. This type of communicator is the easiest to communicate with as they can remain level-headed in disagreement and are not forceful in any way. They are not trying to enforce an attitude of superiority, nor are they trying to stay hidden. They stand in interaction as they are and are not trying too hard to be anything they are not. People respect the fact that this communicator can

There is not necessarily one of these best styles, but some may be more effective than others in different situations. There may be some situations where communicating more passively is required, and somewhere a more balanced, assertive style is the best choice. Being honest with ourselves and recognizing which style we use the most can help us to analyze our interactions and see why people may react to us in one way or another. Awareness is the key to changing anything. Choosing the most effective communication style will allow you to see other people's true personalities instead of seeing their reaction to your communication style choice. Being aware of the different styles and how they look can help you choose which one to use and when. These all come with their different body language, and understanding them can help you determine which of the styles you use and which style other people use. Knowing this may help you analyze their intentions. If someone approaches you with an aggressive communication style, you can glean that they do not have much interest in what you may have to contribute to the discussion and maybe quite forceful with their words. Knowing the different styles can help you to avoid being offended and hurt if someone approaches you in this way.

As we have learned, communicating with other people involves much more than just speaking. It involves listening well, reading and demonstrating specific body language, analyzing personality types, and communicating effectively with your words. It may seem like a lot goes into a simple conversation, and while this is true, with practice, in time, you will become the most effective communicator you have ever been.

CHAPTER 4
Emotional Intelligence In The Workplace

Emotional intelligence is especially important when it comes to professional relationships. Emotional intelligence is a trait that is highly sought after by employers all over the world. Emotional intelligence has grown in importance over the years, especially when it comes to the workplace. Just because you walk into your workplace does not mean that all your emotions you felt that day get automatically put away. Although it often appears that way to most people, in reality, emotions are always existent in the workplace, but they are normally kept in check to remain professional. People often pretend that they do not have emotions during work hours to avoid appearing unprofessional.

In society today, emotional intelligence is very important because of how workplace culture is different. Nowadays, most work is done in teams and not as individuals. Forward-thinking employers realize that acknowledging emotions in the workplace tend to build better working environments. Realizing this would mean that people have to be more aware and conscious of other people's feelings along with their own. People who have better emotional intelligence are more adaptable to change, which is a required skill in today's fast-paced environment.

Professional relationships are one of the most common types of relationships with which people struggle. The reason for this is because of how unique it is to the other different types of relationships. If we think about friendships, familial relationships, and romantic relationships, the common element between these three is a level of closeness. When it comes to professional relationships, it is almost forbidden to nurture that sense of closeness. When two people in a professional relationship grow close, it may evolve into a friendship that overpowers the professional relationship.

Many people have to re-learn their communication skills and techniques solely for professional relationships. Although there isn't a universal mandate for how people should communicate in professional environments, there is a loose structure of how people should act. So why do people give professional relationships so much importance? Why do people take courses or read books on how to build better professional relationships?

The simple answer is that humans are naturally social creatures; we crave positive interactions and friendship as much as we crave food and water. So it does make a lot of sense that the better the relationships we have at work, the happier and more productive we will feel. What's more important is that good professional relationships give people more freedom. Rather than spending time and energy dealing with problems caused by negative relationships, we can simply just focus on our work and opportunities. Good professional relationships are also extremely necessary if you are hoping to develop your career. If your boss or manager doesn't trust you or even like you, then it is highly unlikely that he/she will consider you for a promotion. Overall, people want to work with people whom they are on good terms with.

The Benefits of High EI in the Workplace

Despite the critique, emotional intelligence is a concept that heavily appeals to the general public. There is even more appeal for this topic in certain industries. Many companies have recently incorporated personality assessments as a part of job application processes to identify those who have higher EI. The level of a person's emotional intelligence indicates that this person would make a better team member or leader.

Those in industries where their success highly relies on their ability to perform tend to showcase better emotional intelligence due to more practice from exercising it every day. For example, people in sales tend to showcase more self-discipline than other occupations because of the targets that they have to meet. People within the sales industry are normally hired due to their motivation to make money.

Due to this motivation, they likely have a goal or target in mind, including the amount they want to sell in a certain time frame. By having a defined goal, this person is driven to do everything they can to reach it and is constantly overcoming obstacles like instant gratification and laziness. If a person is constantly overcoming those obstacles every day, those obstacles slowly start to feel like they aren't there anymore. That's when self-discipline becomes a habit. Keep this in mind, as it is the goal that I want us to get to throughout this book.

Further, we have learned that people with high emotional intelligence possess a high level of optimism and resilience to negativity. This skill represents another one of the numerous benefits of high emotional intelligence in the workplace. Research studies have found that optimists tend to be more successful compared to pessimists. There was a research study that focused on the success of a few salespeople. They found that the more optimistic salespeople made 88% more sales than the pessimistic salespeople. They found that optimistic salespeople were less likely to quit their jobs or give up during stressful work times. They were also more likely to describe a positive future when it came to their sales careers. This result makes a lot of sense. Having a more positive mindset at work prevents you from giving up and motivates you to work harder. Those who try harder than others and refuse to give up will be more successful than those that give up at the first hint of failure.

How Understanding Others' Emotions Will Benefit You in the Workplace

- It will help you to manage your employees.

Leaders in the workplace with higher emotional intelligence tend to have happier employees, which lower major costs like attrition and increase overall workplace productivity. As discussed earlier, people who have higher emotional intelligence tend to live a happier life outside of the workplace due to a lower risk of disorders like depression and anxiety.

- It will help you to work as a team with your co-workers.

Working as a team is essential in the workplace, and understanding others' emotions will prove extremely helpful in working as a team.

- It will lead to a better overall working environment.

Being able to understand other people's emotions is crucial to maintaining a positive and supportive workplace environment. Having a high level of EI will lead to a positive working environment.

- It will lead to ease of adapting to changes.

By better understanding others and having a high level of EI, you will adapt to changes as they come and employ them in your working life.

- Having greater self-control will lead to fewer conflicts in the workplace.

By controlling yourself, you will choose moments to share your opinions and use the most productive ways for conflict resolution.

- It will lead to greater overall success.

Having a higher level of emotional intelligence will help you to get the most out of your interactions. Instead of wondering if someone is truthful, or if they were only pretending to be interested in the conversation you just had, you will know as soon as they begin talking. Sometimes you will know even before they say a word. You will know how to recruit people for your team and get them on board with your message.

How to Show High EI in the Workplace

In our professional relationships, we often want to be the most aware of how we come across, and how we say or do not say will be interpreted. Because everyone will usually try to be on their best behavior in a professional setting, they are unlikely to ask for clarification if their feelings are hurt or think we have said something to offend them. In this situation, we would want to employ the techniques we learned to ensure that we can anticipate how other people see us. These techniques will also give the other person enough time to share and speak and ensure that we are making comfortable eye contact not to seem creepy or uninterested. These relationships are more distant than any other and are the ones that often come at a high price if there is a misunderstanding. We want to maintain these relationships even though we may not care deeply for the people themselves. Compared to the other types of relationships, these will not come naturally as we cannot always act on our instincts when communicating with these people. Communicating in relationships like these takes practice and exposing yourself to more and more professional interactions. These interactions can include; networking or workplace events that will help you better use those techniques you learned to improve your professional relationships.

How to Use High EI to get a Promotion

By learning to read people better, you can advance your life in more ways than not. For instance, if you seek promotion from your boss, you may be able to read their body language, verbal and non-verbal messages, and their overall mood to determine if it's the right time to ask for a promotion or a raise. Or at a lower level, you can determine what more they want to see from you to gain a promotion.

To further illustrate this concept, we are going to look at a case study.

Two employees perform the same role in a corporate office environment. One of them is confident and self-assured. He walks into the office with his head held high and is quite talkative. He has a good rapport with most office workers, and he maintains a positive work environment. When he takes a phone call, people can hear him throughout the office as he speaks at a high volume and with a deep voice. The other employee is an extremely hard worker. He is quiet and shy, but he gets to work on time each day, and he works silently with a focus all day long. He has never taken a sick day in his two years at this company and often works through lunch. He has not had many one-on-one conversations with his boss as he works in a self-directed manner and does not need much guidance. Which of these two employees will get the promotion?

While most people would like to believe that hard work demonstrates knowledge and skill, and this will show itself, the silent hard worker who lacks confidence more often than not goes unnoticed. While it is a shame, in most cases, we cannot focus all of our time on our work to show our bosses that we deserve the next promotion. Our employers want to see the ability to work a room to display our knowledge engagingly. While the second worker silently devotes himself to his work, his boss notices the more confident and more demonstrative employee. The first employee makes a point to start conversations with him each morning and tell him the latest work-related knowledge. As unfortunate as it may be, we must be able to make ourselves noticed. Doing this involves using our body language to our benefit. If we seem reserved and shy, people will not entrust us with representing the company's image at a conference, for example. The employee who demonstrates confident body language, including a confident tone of voice, will gain listeners over the quiet but knowledgeable employee. We must work on the balance of confidence and skill to progress to where we want to be.

CHAPTER 5
Emotional Intelligence In Your Relationships

We frequently use the term 'relationship' in psychology and multiple languages all over the world. Relationships are defined as 'how two or more concepts, objects, or people are connected, or the state of connected.' When people think 'relationship,' they always automatically think about the romantic kind. Although that is the one that jumps to mind when we hear that word, there are numerous types of relationships. We can pretty much sum it up to just four kinds, but there are hundreds of different styles of relationships if we wanted to get specific. This chapter will be studying the relationships between people and how we can improve them using emotional intelligence.

Different Types of Relationships

When it comes to the topic of relationships, most people don't know what they're doing. Most people feel exhilarated during the early stages of a romantic relationship. Still, as they get back into their regular daily routine, their baggage begins to reveal itself, and people often find themselves amid escalating conflict, hurt feelings, emotional withdrawal, insufficient coping techniques, or just plain boredom. There is no denying that maintaining a healthy and happy relationship is a difficult task. Luckily for us, a growing field of research focused on relationships and emotional intelligence that provides us with science-based solutions and guidance into building healthy habits to foster the happiest relationships. We build relationships of not only love but hard work and communication. We will be learning about the fundamental lessons that are simple but difficult to master regarding relationships and how emotional intelligence can improve them.

Friendships

Friendship is when two people have a close association marked by feelings of respect, care, concern, admiration, and love. We describe the primary defining characteristic of friendship as a preference for a specific person. Keep in mind, however, that different types of people have their definitions and requirements for friendship. For instance, young children may refer to someone as their 'best friend' within the first five minutes of meeting them, but people from more reserved cultures or simply people who are just shyer, have reported that they have only had a few friends during their whole life.

There is not only one definition of what a friendship constitutes or doesn't constitute. However, these are the most common traits of friendship:

- Both people have a desire for regular contact with one another. We define regular contact once a year or once every two days.
- There is some degree of commitment, whether it's to the friendship itself or both people's well-being.
- There is mutual trust, compassion, and concern.
- These two people share common hobbies, interests, beliefs, and opinions.
- These two people share knowledge about one another's interests, loves, fears, or emotions.
- These two people both share feels of respect, love, appreciation, or admiration of each other.

Familial Relationships

Familial relationships refer to the relationships that people have with their families. Although the family is just one single word, it has numerous different meanings. People often have their way of defining what family means to them. The definition of family is different based on the person's cultural, economic, and social standing. However, what family has in common with everyone is that the people who are calling other people's families are making it clear that those people are critical to them in some way, thus, identifying them as family.

The definition of family is 'a fundamental social group in society, typically consisting of one or two parents and their children.' Although this definition is a perfect start point, numerous family structures are more modern and excluded by this definition. Modern family structures could include couples that don't have children or other varieties of a family unit. Another meaning of family is "two or more people who share goals and values, have long-term commitments to one another, and usually reside in the same dwelling." This definition better encompasses the majority of more modern family units. Throughout the book, we will be using this definition to relate to the topics we will discuss.

So what makes a family a family? The traditional making of a family consists of a mother, father, and children. This type of family is the type that we usually see on TV shows and movies. However, in the modern world, families are shown in many different varieties, which are very different from the traditional kind that most people imagine. In the present day, many children are brought up in homes by a single parent, their grandparents, or same-sex parents. Some families choose not to have children or cannot have children due to a medical or emotional reason. The idea that two parents and children make a family is the most basic form of the definition. For us to better understand family relationships, we must use a broader definition. In addition to this more general form of the definition, many people in society today consider their friends to be family or their pets to be family.

Professional Relationships

A professional relationship is very much different than the close relationships we just learned about, like friendships and familial relationships. A professional relationship is an ongoing interaction between two individuals who follow established boundaries deemed appropriate under their governing standards. The ability to develop professional relationships is the backbone of a person's career development.

Professional relationships consist of many different types. The most common one that people may think of is their relationship with their manager or boss. Or if you are that manager or boss, then professional relationships are the ones you have with your employees. However, professional relationships have many more types than that. Think doctor to patient relationships, lawyer to client, teacher to student, a service provider to the customer, and so on. Professional relationships function in a manner that is very different from friendships and family relationships. Although most professional relationships still have a vital friendliness element, not many people would consider their doctor their 'friend.'

Romantic Relationships

Romantic relationships are the kind of relationship that is heavily portrayed all over our media. As we mentioned before, this type of relationship in western culture holds more value than other relationships. Traditional romantic relationships are generally between a man and a woman. Although this structure is very outdated now, we modernly describe romantic relationships as when two people consensually agree to be exclusively in a relationship together where passionate love is shared. In our modern-day, these relationships can exist between a man and a woman, a man and a man, a woman and a woman, and other gender structure varieties.

On top of that, there are also different types of romantic relationships. Love isn't one-size-fits-all. It means something different to every single person, but it also feels and looks different to everyone. It is for this reason that there are so many different types of romantic relationships. These expanded definitions allow every person to find the best fit for their personality, lifestyle, and love concept.

Healthy Versus Unhealthy Relationships

To learn about evolving unhealthy relationships into healthy ones, we must first understand a healthy relationship. Although different types of relationships have different standards of healthiness, they all follow a similar guideline. To make things simple, we will focus on a healthy romantic relationship within this subchapter.

The couple needs to have three things to have a healthy romantic relationship; healthy communication, healthy boundaries, and healthy relationship boosters. Honest, open, and safe communication is crucial when it comes to having a healthy relationship. The first step into building one is to make sure both people understand each other's needs and expectations. The two people have to be on the same page; this is very important. For two people to be on the same page, they must always be communicating. Most healthy relationships follow these five components:

- **Speaking up:** When a relationship is healthy, the relationship people are comfortable talking about a problem rather than holding it in.
- **Respect:** In a healthy relationship, each person values the other's wishes and feelings. They let each other know when they are making an effort to keep their best interests in mind. Having mutual respect is an essential part of having a healthy relationship.
- **Compromise:** Arguments or disagreements are normal in healthy relationships; this means that learning to compromise when two people disagree on something is important. People in healthy relationships solve the conflict in a healthy way, using compromises to satisfy both parties.
- **Support:** Healthy relationships are all about supporting each other and not putting each other down. Two people in a relationship should always be offering encouragement and reassurance to one another. It is also essential to let each other know when one needs support.
- **Privacy:** Healthy relationships require space and personal time for both parties. Just because two people are in a relationship doesn't mean that they always need to be together or share everything.

Below is a list of situations that exhibit unhealthy behaviors in a relationship:

- Your partner gets jealous or angry when you talk to someone else.
- Your partner is always calling and texting you to check on who you are with and where you are.
- Your partner can get physically threatening or verbally aggressive.
- Your partner puts you down, makes you feel bad, or calls you bad names.
- Your partner uses threats, bargains, or even force to make you do things that you don't want to do.

- Your partner threatens to harm your property, pets, friends, and family.
- Your partner controls your behavior and tells you how to behave and what to do.
- You know that they are not the significant others you want/need, but you are under the impression that you can change them.
- You stay with this person because you think it is better than being alone.
- Physical intimacy is the primary essential thing in the relationship.
- They are the sole decision-maker regarding what to do and where to go.
- You guys argue all the time.
- They always make fun of you or put you down.
- You are embarrassed when you hang out in public with your partner.
- You don't have time for anyone or anything else.
- When you are with your friends, they humiliate you or ignore you.
- You can't talk about contraception or safe sex.
- They bad mouth your family.
- They tell you what to wear and what to do.
- They tell people things about you that are bad and not true.

The Benefits of High EI in Relationships

Having a high level of EI will help your relationships in numerous ways. In addition to the conflict resolution skills that it will bring you, it will also lead to a better ability to connect with other people.

Having a better social life as an optimistic person is probably evident at this point. People typically want to be around other positive people and often avoid those who are negative. Naturally, most people want to spend their time with optimistic people as they tend to be more cheerful and upbeat. They make better supporters and help encourage their friends to be better versions of themselves. Negative people tend to have a negative outlook on their own life, extending over to having a negative perspective on other people's lives. Generally, most people don't want to spend time with those who bring them down and make them feel negative about their own life. Even negative people prefer to spend time with positive people. Having more positive thinking allows you to attract other positive thinkers to generate motivation and inspiration to achieve bigger and better things in life.

CHAPTER 6
Increasing Your Level Of Emotional Intelligence Part 1- Motivation

This chapter will begin looking at strategies that will help you increase your level of emotional intelligence. We will spend the next five chapters of this book looking at a plan for strengthening each of the components of emotional intelligence to understand better how to begin changing your life.

Why Should You Increase Your Level of Emotional Intelligence?

We will spend the next five chapters of this book, looking at strategies for strengthening each emotional intelligence component. In this chapter, we are going, beginning with motivation.

Remember from the first chapter of this book when we discussed the factors contributing to a person's emotional intelligence? We will review them here first before moving on.

The following components make up emotional intelligence:

- **Self-Awareness:**

Self-awareness allows people to understand their strengths and weaknesses. Self-awareness gives people a better understanding of how to react appropriately to other people and in certain situations. When a person reflects on their emotions, they begin to gain self-awareness. To grow emotional intelligence, a person will need to think about their feelings and how they most often react in negative situations. When a person becomes more aware of which emotions they are dealing with, they can begin to manage and control them appropriately, leading to a higher self-awareness level.

- **Self-Regulation:**

When a person has self-regulation, high EI comes into play by allowing the person to properly regulate their emotions to keep it in check when needed.

- **Motivation:**

People that have high emotional intelligence tend to have more motivation, which makes them more optimistic. Having more optimism causes them to have more resilience towards negativity.

- **Empathy:**

Usually, people who are more successful in connecting with others exhibit strong traits of empathy and compassion.

- **Social Skills:**

Likely a person with high emotional intelligence has the social skills needed to showcase their respect and care for others. Those who have higher EI tend to get along better with people in general for this reason.

Motivation

Motivation is one of the components of emotional intelligence, and we are going to spend this chapter looking at what motivation is and how to increase your motivation.

People often have the wrong mindset where they think that they need to feel entirely motivated before they start working on a task/job. This mindset is unrealistic. People's motivation often does not arrive until they have started that task and are beginning to see progress.

When people see progress, they start to see the fruits of their labor, and they become even more motivated to keep working until they have completed their task. You might be wondering about the motivation you need to start working altogether. The answer to this is the following; A person must understand the 'why' in the first place. Before you even begin working on it, you should know what the benefits are going to be. You would be surprised at how many people waste a lot of time doing work they do not need to complete.

Moreover, people should be using prioritization to get the most urgent and important work out of the way first. By understanding the benefits of completing a task or job, you will fully estimate its importance. In terms of smaller tasks/jobs, simply understanding the benefits of completing that task should be enough for motivation. For larger tasks and jobs, you must have a way to measure your progress to gain motivation and confidence from your work further.

One main reason people put off doing the work they need to do is that they subconsciously find that their work is too overwhelming. Start by just breaking down whatever that task is into littler parts and then focus on one at a time. If you find yourself still wanting to procrastinate after you've already broken it down, then break it down even more. You will eventually get to a point where the task you need to do is so easy that you would feel very badly about yourself if you didn't just do it. If you are struggling with motivation, this is a great way to cope, as it can help you put one foot in front of the other and get started so that your motivation will begin to grow as you begin to see results.

What Is Motivation?

Motivation links closely with willpower, so we will begin by discussing the relationship between motivation and willpower. The bottom line of willpower is achieving long-term goals by resisting temporary temptations and urges. To do this, you have to have the motivation to achieve those goals in the first place; otherwise, you would not care about reaching them.

People report that the biggest obstacle for people achieving change in their lives was the lack of willpower. Even though many people often blame the scarcity of their willpower for their unhealthy choices, they are still grasping on to the hope of achieving it one day. Most people in this study also reported that they think willpower can be taught and learned. They are correct. Weak willpower isn't the only reason for a person to fail at achieving their goals. Psychologists in the field of willpower have built three crucial components when it comes to achieving goals.

Psychologists said that you first need to set a clear goal and then establish the motivation for change. Psychologists also said the second component was to monitor your behavior regarding that goal. Willpower itself is the third and final component. If your goal is similar to the following; stop smoking, get fit, study more, or stop wasting time on the internet, willpower is an important concept to understand if you are looking to achieve any of those goals. If a person does not have goals or has them but has no motivation to achieve them, they are more likely to live a stagnant and unfulfilling life.

For this reason, having a goal is not enough; you need motivation and willpower to achieve those goals. Having motivation and willpower is a trait that people with high emotional intelligence possess. They can exercise strong willpower and strong motivation to achieve their goals. They can use this emotional intelligence to reflect on their lives, set goals for themselves, and then push themselves to achieve those goals.

The Relationship Between Motivation and Emotional Intelligence

The relationship that motivation has to emotional intelligence is threefold. The first is that having a high level of emotional intelligence will bring you more motivation. Thus, increasing your emotional intelligence will bring you motivation. The second is that people who have more motivation and a higher level of emotional intelligence are more optimistic. The third is that people who are more optimistic and have a higher level of emotional intelligence tend to be more resilient to negativity.

The Benefits of Optimism and Resiliency

As you know, another benefit of having motivation, and thus a high level of emotional intelligence is that you are much more likely to be optimistic and resilient to negativity. In this section, we will look at some of the benefits of optimism to give you a better idea of the numerous ways that emotional intelligence can benefit your life.

Numerous research studies have recently found that positive thinking brings many benefits to a person's health. It can reduce a person's stress levels, improve their mental health and physical health. a positive mindset will also help you build more realistic expectations of yourself and others.

A lot of negative people spread the belief that they cannot change things. They believe that no matter how much you try to improve your skills, your talent will always be the limiting factor.

Rather than letting these negative people spread their negative mindsets about whether or not you can achieve something, being resilient to negativity will help you ignore comments like these and maintain your inner peace. Below are some tips for remaining resilient;

- Expect to need help from others at some point. Achieving goals without the help of others is often unrealistic, especially if your goals are big. Instead, replace it with the mindset that you will likely require help along the way. This change in mindset will motivate you to build stronger relationships with people.
- Expect failure along the way. A person can't smoothly achieve their goals. Everyone experiences failure along the way. Accept that fact now, so you aren't surprised by that truth later on.

    An important concept I want you to understand is that failures are welcome when you are practicing self-discipline. Do not begin your journey of increasing emotional intelligence, thinking that you don't experience failure. This kind of thinking is only going to discourage you from picking yourself back up. There will be days when you stay in bed instead of going to the gym or when you decide to eat a double cheeseburger instead of choosing a healthier option. Having failures is entirely okay as long as you learn from it and find a way to overcome it next time around.

    The best way to overcome failure is to prevent it in the first place. If you are going to buy some dinner, don't go to a restaurant that offers unhealthy options. Go to one that ONLY provides healthy options, so you have to pick from their selection. If you plan to go to the gym in the morning, call your workout buddy and ask them to come with you to the gym. That way, you won't want to stand them up, so you'll be forced to go.

    By accepting this fact before they arise, you will not be surprised, but rather you will feel prepared.

    Before you begin, take some time to write in your journal. Write about what some of the possible obstacles may be. Once you have done this, take some time to plan and decide how you will deal with them when they arise, so that they do not disrupt your progress or cause you to resort to old ways that are unhealthy.

    By setting yourself up for success in this way, you will be able to tackle any challenge that comes your way, without having your new lifestyle jeopardized.

- Expect to have to improve your skills and abilities. Don't be under the impression that your goals are achievable by remaining the

same way you are now. If it is a big goal, it will likely require you to learn new skills or develop existing ones.
- Expect the goal to change your reality when you reach it.

Just because someone reached their biggest goal does not mean their life will be perfect afterward. The person's reality will change, which means they will face new problems and obstacles; this is normal.

The Importance of Removing Negativity

The most effective method is to stay away from negative people simply. To do this, you have to be able to identify who these negative people are. Below, we will look at the things we have to look out to identify negative people.

How to Identify and Remove Negative People From Your Life

1. Negative people are always complaining.
Negative people tend to express their negativity frequently verbally. They convince themselves that the world is out to get them. They can find something to complain about at any time. It can be something as simple as the weather, work responsibilities, or just an encounter of bad luck. Negative people aren't able to take a step back and look at other factors around them.
2. Negative people have a negative view of the outside world.
Negative people struggle to see the good in the world. A famous quote by Albert Einstein stated that "There are two ways to live your life. One is as though nothing is a miracle. The other is as though everything is a miracle." Negative people are the ones that never see any miracles in the world.
3. Negative people expect the worst from life.
Negative people enjoy anticipating the worst. A negative person's mindset is always one where they need to feel alert and protected at all times. Their mindset is that if they expect the worst-case scenario, they won't be as disappointed when it happens.
4. Negative people always act like victims.
Although everybody is prone to complaining about something in their lives, most people can pull themselves together and make a better situation. Negative people are different because their self-pity is not temporary; it is long-lasting. They are often familiar with illnesses, traumas, or crises because they are always assuming that life is a fight that they will lose.
5. Negative people have thin skin and are easily offended.
Negative people are very sensitive towards any type of criticism and can even perceive a compliment as an insult. They will often interpret

innocent comments as the other person 'being rude' where a positive person would not have overanalyzed the comment. This perception makes negative people struggle with relationships as they are always expecting the worst from the other person.

6. Negative people are never positive or upbeat.

A negative person tends to miss out on all the positive things in life. They rarely can recognize or even enjoy excitement, passion, or joy because they never feel these emotions. When a person fixates on all the negative aspects of their life, relationships, and jobs, it is difficult for them to feel positive or upbeat.

7. Negative people are a stream of constant complaints.

A complaint means where a person wishes that something was different in their life. This wish could be small, like having misplaced their keys, or it could be a larger complaint like being mistreated by their boss. Even if their complaints are justified, it still means that they aren't getting their way. Negative people always feel like they aren't getting their way, so they find many things to complain about.

8. Negative people think that everyone else is wrong and that they are always right.

Negative people often feel as if they are the smartest people on earth. They feel as if everyone else is not as intelligent as them. However, what they cannot see is that if everyone is always in the wrong, the problem might lie within themselves and not the millions of other people. Negative people don't realize that they aren't the smartest people on earth.

9. Negative people have bad reputations due to their attitude.

It is fairly easy for positive people to sense the bad energy from negative people. They often pick up on their attitudes quite quickly. However, it may be more difficult for you to pick up the signs if you are a recovering negative person. Luckily, negative people usually build a bad reputation for themselves, making it easier for you to figure out who to avoid.

10. Negative people dwell on bad news.

Negative people love talking to others about the most recent bad news. However, overexposure to bad news affects people very deeply, according to recent research. Studies have found that frequent media exposure to tragedy and violence contributes to people's PTSD, anxiety, or depression and can further influence a more negative view of someone's life.

Tips for Increasing Motivation

If you are unsure of your motive or your "why," take some time to look deep within yourself and address the reasons why you are reading this book or the reasons why you feel it is time to make a change in your life. By taking stock of your feelings, will lead you to find your motivation for seeking change.

Whatever your objective, writing it down will help to solidify it and make it more real. By having it written down on paper, you will have put your reason for doing all of this out into the universe, and it will make you feel as if there is no going back now. Putting it into the universe will keep you motivated when times get tough. You can revisit that paper anytime you need a reminder of why you are taking on such a challenge. Seeing that paper will remind you of why it is all worth it.

When you find it hard to understand the social cues someone is sending you, or when you are in conflict with someone, having your "why" written down will re-inspire you to continue. Writing it down will enable you to keep going even when you feel it is difficult, which will lead to lasting changes. When it comes to mindset, being aware of your motivation is extremely beneficial.

More Tips for Increasing Motivation

Let's take a look at some other ways to create motivation in your life so that you can increase your level of emotional intelligence. Below are nine steps that you should follow to increase your motivation in 9 days. These steps work by helping you begin changing your life in positive ways, creating motivation for you to make further changes.

Step 1: Reflect on your Shortcomings.
Everyone has shortcomings. They could range from being uncomfortable with reading other people to forgetting the names of people you have met. Regardless of what it is, it has a similar effect on everyone. The first step to mastering your self-discipline is acknowledging your shortcomings, no matter what they might be. People often try to pretend that their weaknesses don't exist to portray themselves as a strong person. Lying to yourself in this way is extremely ineffective when it comes to self-discipline. The purpose of acknowledging your weaknesses is not to make yourself feel bad; instead, it helps you recognize what they are and help you plan to overcome them. Acknowledge your flaws; it is impossible to overcome them until you do this.

Step 2: Set Goals
To continue strengthening your self-discipline, a person must have a clear vision of what goals they are trying to accomplish. They must also have an understanding of what success means to them. If a person doesn't know where they're planning to go or what accomplishing their goals even and Tails, it is easy for them to lose their way or get sidetracked.

Make sure the goals that you are setting have a clear and concise purpose. For example, don't use goals like "I want to be rich by the next five years." This goal is too broad for it to have a strong meaning. Instead, you should make a goal that is quantifiable like "I am planning on saving $20,000 by the end of this year". Then, when you have a quantifiable goal, you can make a plan that makes sense for yourself. A person can plan to save $2,000 per month over the next year to hit their goal of saving $20,000 by the end of the year. They can break down these goals even further and figure out where they can save money or how they can make more money to accomplish that goal in their budget.

Step 3: Discipline Yourself

Self-discipline is not something that people are born with; it is mostly a learned behavior. Self-discipline is just like any other skill that people may be looking to grow; it requires repetition and daily practice. Like going to the gym, the more you work out your muscles, the bigger and stronger they will become. Changes do not happen overnight; instead, to strengthen your muscles and grow them, it will take at least several weeks for a person to see their progress. The effort and focus that training self-discipline requires can be extremely tiring.

The more time you practice self-discipline, the more it can become difficult to keep utilizing your willpower. Sometimes when a person faces a big temptation or decision, they may feel that overcoming that large temptation makes it harder for them to overcome other tasks requiring self-discipline. The only way to move past this is to have a good mindset. By having a good mindset, it creates a buffer for how quickly your willpower becomes drained. Also, like the muscle example we used, by exerting your willpower more often, you will have a higher tolerance and therefore be able to exert it more than if you were just starting.

Step 4: Make it a Habit.

To strengthen self-discipline, you need to instill a new habit, which can feel very intimidating at first, especially if you are focusing on the entire goal all at once. To avoid this daunting feeling, keep it very simple. Break your bigger goal into smaller doable ones. Instead of trying to accomplish one huge goal all at once or to change all of your habits, focus on doing just one thing consistently, and exercise your self-discipline with that one small thing.

For example, if you are looking to get into better shape, start by exercising for 10 to 15 minutes per day. Instead of trying to go to the gym for 2 hours every day, which can be very daunting, start with a smaller goal in mind first. By taking baby steps, you can get your mind used to that habit and slowly increase the amount of time you spend at the gym. Eventually, once you feel like that goal has become a habit, you can then begin to focus on other small goals and keep building up words from there.

Step 5: Change your Lifestyle

In the earlier chapters, we learned that glucose levels play a big role in a person's brain power, which controls a person's willpower. The sensation of being hungry can cause people to feel angry, annoyed, and irritated. This feeling is real, and everyone has felt it before, and often has a huge impact on a person's willpower. Research has found evidence that having low blood sugar weakens a person's ability to make good decisions.

When a person is hungry, their ability to concentrate suffers a lot, and their brains don't function optimally. Therefore, a person's self-control is likely to be weakened when their body is in this state. To prevent this, make sure to be eating small meals constantly to prevent yourself from feeling that annoying hungry feeling that causes people to have a lapse in judgment. Since exercising willpower takes up a lot of energy from a person's brain, make sure to keep fuelling it with enough glucose so that the brain can keep functioning at an optimal level.

Step 6: Change your mind

In the earlier chapters, we learned that a person's point of view or their beliefs could create a buffer of how long it takes to have their willpower drained completely. Although most researchers believe that there is a limit to how much we can tap into our willpower, they also found that the people who believe that there wasn't a limit had a bigger will power stockpile. If a person believes that they have a limited amount of willpower, they probably will not surpass those limits. However, if a person does not place a strict limit on themselves, they are less likely to use up their willpower stockpile before meeting their goals.

A person's internal perception about their willpower and self-control plays a huge role in determining how much willpower they have. If a person can remove these obstacles by believing that they have a large stockpile of willpower and believing in themselves, they are less likely to drain out their willpower than someone who believes that they don't have much of it. So try changing your perception of how you see your willpower. Try to think of it as a source that can run out, but you have a larger amount of it because of your beliefs. This mindset is a much better mindset than thinking that willpower will run out, so you should be stingy with it.

Step 7: Have a Backup

Many psychologists use a famous technique that helps with boosting willpower called "implementation intention." This technique is where you give yourself a plan when you face a potentially difficult situation. We will now look at an example. If a person is trying to reduce the amount of alcohol they drink and they know that they are going to a party where others will ask if they want to drink alcohol, instead of asking for a beer like they normally would, they will instead ask for a plain soda with lime. By making a plan before going into a situation where you know you will face big temptations, you will have an action plan where you can automatically use rather than have to come up with an excuse on the spot and risk failure. When a person goes into those situations with a plan, it helps give them the mindset and self-control necessary to overcome obstacles. They will save energy by not having to make sudden decisions or make sudden plans based on their emotional state. Saving energy will make them less likely to cave into temptations and more likely to exercise their self-discipline.

Step 8: Reward
Like anything else in life, it is necessary to give yourself a break and reward yourself. Give yourself something to look forward to by planning an appropriate reward when you accomplish your goals. This kind of rewarding yourself is not much different from when you were a little kid, and you got a treat from your parents for showing good behavior. When a person has something to look forward to, it gives them the extra motivation to succeed.
Anticipation is a powerful thing. It gives people something to focus on so that they are not only thinking of all the things they need to change. When you have achieved one of your goals, you can find yourself a new goal and a new reward to keep motivating yourself to move forward. However, the reward should not be something unhealthy. For example, in the previous example of the person trying to lower their alcohol intake, their reward for not drinking as often should not be that they will go binge drinking next Friday. Their awards should be something healthy that won't make them lose progress on all the work that they've done.
Step 9: Forgive
Even if a person has all the best intentions and the most well-made plans, sometimes they will fall short when practicing self-discipline. Avoiding failure altogether is impossible, and we should not build a mindset around that. Everyone will have their ups and downs, their successes, and their failures. The key to overcoming the failures that you will face is simply to keep moving forward. If you stumble on your journey of self-discipline, instead of giving up altogether, acknowledge what caused it, learn from it, and then move on. Don't let yourself get caught up in frustration, anger, or guilt because these emotions are the ones that will de-motivate you and get in the way of your future progress. Learn from the mistakes you have made and be comfortable with forgiving yourself. Once you have done that, you can get your head back in the game and start where you left off.

CHAPTER 7
Increasing Your Level Of Emotional Intelligence Part 2- Your Emotions And Needs

This chapter will continue to look at how you can increase your emotional intelligence by talking about your emotions and how it will benefit you to begin acknowledging and understanding them.

Reflecting on and Understanding Your Emotions

When a person reflects on their emotions, they begin to gain self-awareness. To grow emotional intelligence, start by thinking about your feelings and how you react to negative situations. When you become more aware of which emotions you are dealing with, you can begin to manage and control them appropriately.

Listening to Feelings

A critical step in increasing your emotional intelligence is to state your feelings and listen to other people say theirs. This exchange of emotions can be in the face of conflict, but it does not have to be. Exchanging feelings in this way is a useful tool when looking to resolve disputes. When stating your feelings, you are usually going to be talking about how something made you feel. People tend to shut down and become defensive when something makes them feel a certain way, so being open and honest enough to state your feelings about something takes practice and bravery. However, before you can do that, you need to know how to read your emotions.

How To Do This

- Observe: Once you have started being more self-aware, try to understand your behavior better. Begin to observe your emotions and pay attention to them.
- Pause for a moment: Stop to think about what emotions you feel before you act. It may be challenging to do this in emotionally heated situations, but it will become a habit with practice.

How to Begin Listening to Your Inner Feelings

Knowing how to listen to your feelings is essential in being able to increase your emotional intelligence. For many people, this is a challenge. We live in a world where looking inward and getting in touch with the deeper parts of yourself is not as valued as distracting yourself is. Needing to distract ourselves is primarily due to the media and consumerism, which constantly bombards us with information, so tuning out of all of this feels nice. Also, objects and activities for distraction are sold to us everywhere we go. Looking inward and getting in touch with your feelings will take practice, but it will become easier once you get used to it. There are different ways to do this, and I will outline one of them here for you.

- **Commit to Doing So**

The first step to listening to your feelings is committing to doing so. If you do not commit, it will prove difficult for you to examine yourself without a barrier there. Once you begin listening to your feelings, you will be able to improve the things that make you feel negative emotions, and the first step to doing this is noticing what those emotions are.

- **Notice Sensations In Your Body**

Once you have committed to looking deep within yourself, you are ready to begin doing so. The best place to start is to notice when something within you feels different. When we feel emotions, they often manifest themselves somewhere in our bodies. This manifestation usually indicates that you are experiencing some emotion by causing tightness in your chest or a sinking feeling in your stomach. Even if you are not sure what the emotion is, noticing the signs within your body that signal when you feel sentiment is a significant first step.

Many people will feel an emotion and act aggressively through physical aggression or angry words and will never look inward to explore the feeling or what brought it up for them.

Take one second now and notice how your body feels inside. Find any locations of tightness or feelings of unrest within your body. You may be feeling some emotions right now. Bring into your awareness the changes that happen within your body when you experience a feeling so that the next time you feel it, you notice it instead of pushing it away.

- **Give the Feelings a Name**

The next step to listening to your feelings after noticing that you feel something is giving that feeling a name. We are all aware of emotions like fear, anger, happiness, surprise, and sadness. These emotions are an excellent place to begin.

- **Go Deeper**

As we become adults, our emotions become more complicated than the basics- anger, sadness, happiness, and so on. We can experience more profound and more complicated emotions such as shame, anxiety, desperation, shock, doubt, ambiguity, and so on. Once you are comfortable noticing and naming your feelings in a simple way, try to look at them a little deeper and figure out if the emotion you thought was sadness is more disappointment, for example. Suppose you are unsure of what some of these more complex emotions may be. In that case, you can name the feeling in a more straightforward sense (sadness, for example) and then take this word to a thesaurus or an emotion chart online to find other emotions that are related. Seeking out your feelings in this way will help you to describe what you are feeling more precisely.

The Benefits of Understanding Your Own Emotions

Giving yourself a broader vocabulary of emotions will help you to express yourself in more depth so that you can develop a deeper understanding of yourself and others can develop a deeper understanding of you as well. Naming the emotions, you feel when you notice them will allow you to express these emotions to other people in nonviolent communication when the time comes.

Once you are comfortable noticing your feelings, giving them names, and then getting deeper into your exploration of them, you will be able to observe and understand the feelings of others more easily. If you cannot understand your feelings, it will prove quite challenging to understand others' feelings, even if they put them into words for you. Once you know the emotions that you experience, you will be able to relate to someone when they tell you that they feel anxious, for example, as you may have felt this emotion or something similar as you explored your feelings.

The other benefit of understanding your own emotions on a deeper level is that you will understand it better if someone tells you that they feel sad. For example, you may take this deeper in your understanding of emotions by combining this information with the knowledge you have of nonverbal communication (such as body language or facial expressions) to determine that they may be feeling something more complex. You can observe their body language, facial expressions, and the things they have been saying to you in your conversation, combined with them telling you that they feel sad to determine that they may be feeling discouraged or depressed.

By understanding ourselves, we know humans in general and other people with whom we interact.

How to Find a Connection With Yourself

We will look at some ways to connect with yourself to develop your emotional intelligence. We will look at your emotions and your wants, needs, likes, dislikes, and so on. Having this connection with yourself will help you to express yourself in your relationships. Still, it will also help you use nonviolent communication with yourself, which cannot happen without understanding your feelings and needs.

- **Check-In Often**

The first way to find a connection with yourself is to make sure you are taking the time to look inward regularly. If you are not looking, it will be hard to find anything, so the first step is to look.

Checking in with yourself can be as simple as asking, "how am I currently feeling?" This simple question can tell you a lot about your current mental state, physical state, and emotional state, and you may learn things that you didn't even realize you were feeling before looking inward. Make sure you are honest with yourself and listen to what you are feeling.

- **Give Yourself Time and Space**

Sometimes you may find it hard to look inward without becoming distracted or confused, and this is fine as it may take time to become more comfortable with this practice. Giving yourself the time and space to be alone with yourself will help you listen long enough to find the answers. Sometimes, if we are not still enough or do not listen long enough, we miss the answers our bodies are trying to tell us. Ensure that you give yourself the time and space to understand what you are sensing within yourself.

- **Embrace the Answers**

If you are not used to paying attention to your feelings, it may be overwhelming at first. Getting overwhelmed is okay and relatively standard, but the key at this stage is to embrace this and to resist the urge to push them away. Listening to yourself will lead to great things, but it takes courage to listen and let all of your feelings come to the surface. It may be uncomfortable, but pushing through this while being gentle with yourself will lead you to the place where listening to your emotions comes naturally.

- **Journal**

It may be comforting to write any thoughts or feelings you have in a journal. There may be things that you prefer not to vocalize to another person, so writing them down can help you to feel like you have expressed them without having to share them with anyone else. Some things you write may enlighten you to something that you did not know you were feeling.

Once you have found this connection within yourself, maintaining it is essential. Being in touch with yourself is an integral part of using nonviolent communication with yourself and with others. Maintaining a connection with yourself is also crucial for your wellbeing. Being aware of what you feel will let you know when you need to change things that make you feel down or unhappy.

To maintain this connection, the first point, as written above, "check-in often," is what can keep this connection healthy. Just as it is never too late to develop a relationship with yourself and you can do this by checking in, this same technique helps you maintain the connection. No matter how strong a connection a person has with themselves, every person must maintain the relationship and keep it healthy. If you ever feel like your connection with yourself is not as strong as you would like it to be, or that it is not as strong as it once was, you can return to the steps above to regain and re-strengthen that connection.

How to Listen to Your Needs

In this subchapter, we will expand our discussion of feelings by combining it with the topic of needs, as the two are inextricably connected. This aids in emotional intelligence by helping you to begin expressing to others why you feel the way that you feel without judgment. When communicating, one of the most critical parts is recognizing your feelings. As we discussed earlier, when you feel a change in your body, this is likely an emotion that you are experiencing. Most often, specific locations within the body correspond to certain emotions. We feel emotions like anger, anxiety, pride, shame, and fear in the chest and head. We feel emotions like love, happiness, and disgust in the gut. We feel depression and sadness throughout the legs and the arms. Knowing where emotions most often present themselves in the body can help you narrow down your feelings if you are unsure precisely what you feel.

Some needs are associated with feelings that are a facet of raw human emotions. A psychologist who specialized in human necessities concluded that human senses are all associated with human needs. He divided these needs that he researched into different categories, and within each of these categories are several needs. We will look at these needs below.

- **Physiological Needs**

This set of needs is the most basic set of requirements and includes human needs for survival, such as water, air, shelter, food, clothing, sleep, and sex.

- **Safety**

This set of needs is the next most basic, but this is where they become a little more abstract than the previous group's physical needs. These needs include health, employment, personal security, property, and resources.

- **Love & Belonging**

This set of needs are where it becomes less about what humans need to survive with their basic requirements taken care of, and more about those emotional needs. This set of conditions includes family, friendship, intimacy, and a sense of connection.

- **Self-Esteem**

This section is the set of needs that not everyone can have met in their life, but if you are lucky enough to have these met, you are one of the more privileged on earth. These needs are not extras, as they are still considered human necessities, but unfortunately, they are not available to everyone. These needs are status, respect, recognition, self-esteem, freedom, and strength.

- **Self-Actualization**

This section only involves one need, which gives the unit its namesake- self-actualization- or the desire to reach one's full potential in every sense.

Once you can begin to understand your own needs, you can also understand others' needs. Understanding them will help you increase your level of emotional intelligence as it will help you begin gaining a deeper understanding of yourself and others.

CHAPTER 8
Increasing Your Level Of Emotional Intelligence Part 3- Empathy

One of the essential parts of building a higher level of emotional intelligence is by using empathy. In this chapter, we will dive into the concept of empathy and how it will help you increase your emotional intelligence.

What Is Empathy?

Empathy is quite necessary for problem solving and conflict from a place of high emotional intelligence, as it enables you to solve with compassion instead of anger. Before looking at empathy in a broader sense in terms of how it can serve you in your everyday life, we will look at the different types of empathy that exist.

Affective Empathy
Affective empathy is the ability to share someone else's feelings. It is also the ability to understand the feelings of another. It also involves responding according to this shared emotion.

Somatic Empathy
The next type of empathy is called somatic empathy. This type of empathy involves a real, physical reaction to someone else's feelings. For example, if you see that your friend is embarrassed and your face starts to turn red out of second-hand embarrassment.

Cognitive Empathy
The third and final type of empathy is cognitive empathy. This type of empathy is when you can understand another person's feelings to the point of understanding their mental state when feeling that emotion and imagine what they may be thinking or what their thought process may be.

The most common form of empathy, affective empathy (hereafter, empathy), is the ability that a person has to share someone else's feelings. It is also the ability to understand the feelings of another. The difference between empathy and sympathy is that sympathy only involves feeling sorry for someone else's feelings. In contrast, empathy consists of putting yourself in their shoes to feel what they must be feeling.

To give you an idea of what sympathy versus empathy feels like, here is an example. If you have ever had someone open up to you about the emotions they are feeling due to something terrible happening in their lives, did you pity them? Or did you put yourself in their shoes to feel what this terrible event must be making them feel? The former would be sympathy. The latter would be empathy.

Empathy and Emotional Intelligence

Having a high level of emotional intelligence involves being in touch with yourself and the other person (or people) that you are communicating with. To do this, you will need to use empathy. Empathy will help you take responsibility for yourself, your actions, and your reactions and demonstrate a genuine interest in the other person/people. Empathy will help you develop a deeper understanding of the motivations that people have and what they do not say, which inform their actions and reactions. By understanding this, you can connect with people and understand them while helping them understand you.

Empathy is essential because of the way that it gets a person to understand the needs of others. Empathy is beneficial in problem-solving, as well as everyday interactions. Empathetic people express genuine interest in helping others and come from a place of understanding. In interactions with an empathetic person, each person can fully understand and connect with the other person's needs and help them get what they need.

Empathy improves your interactions with others by helping you to solve to the satisfaction of everyone involved. Mutual satisfaction happens because you will be using empathy to understand the other person throughout your interaction. Understanding people will result in empathy being carried on into every other part of your life, which will benefit your relationships and your overall day to day life.

All of our discussion of empathy leads us to compassion. Compassion is a "higher-level emotion," meaning that it requires a person to be wise and more emotionally mature to experience it. Compassion is a form of empathy, meaning that it is a very similar emotion. The difference is that compassion is empathy without being overtaken or overwhelmed by another person's feelings. Further, this means that compassion is the feeling of empathy but a more refined form. The benefit of having compassion is that compassion is an emotion that a person can always feel- in every interaction and with every person. In contrast, empathy can become overwhelming and exhausting if you feel it in every interaction that you have with others.

When thinking about different relationships, are you wondering how you will remain empathetic in every interaction you have with every person? If so, this section holds the answers to your question. Empathy can become very exhausting emotionally if you are always trying to put yourself into other people's shoes and fabricate the emotions they feel to develop a deep understanding of them and what they are going through. For example, when your romantic partner comes home from a hard day at work, you feel their stress and fatigue even if your day was fine. Feeling this can become quite draining for you if you are always having an okay day, and your partner is going through a hard time at work. It is not realistic to think that every day your mood will gravely decline every time you see your partner after work. Taking it on could lead you to feel depressed and resentful eventually. Further, you may wonder why it is not your okay mood that your partner picked up instead. In this situation, compassion becomes the answer. By having compassion for your partner, you can understand deeply that they had a bad day and that they have had many bad days lately, but this does not make your mood decline instantly. Knowing this about your partner, you can exercise compassion by bringing them a cup of tea and sitting with them after putting on their favorite show or making them a nice dinner to cheer them up. In this way, you are aware of their feelings and can understand them, but this does not make you feel the same way as your partner.

Compassion is a more mature form of understanding that comes with time and sometimes with age. This concept is especially relevant for people who tend to be empathetic toward everyone and everything automatically. Changing their empathy into compassion is the key to ensuring that you remain understanding without sacrificing your mental health in the process.

How to Improve Empathy

- Build more empathy by making a point to understand the 'why' behind somebody's emotions or feelings.
- Try to step into the other person's shoes:

Imagine how it would feel to be them in this situation or any given situation.

- Chose to learn from criticism:

Nobody likes criticism, but it is an inevitable part of life. Decide to learn from criticism rather than jumping into defense mode; this way, you can improve your emotional intelligence.

- Practice Honest Self-Expression:

Honest self-expression is what comes as a result of practicing nonviolent communication. The definition of "honest self-expression" is expressing oneself authentically in a way that is likely to inspire compassion in others. Essentially, this is what effective communication entails. Expressing your true feelings and ensuring that the emotions you are expressing are the deepest ones you could find is quite intimidating and can make you feel incredibly vulnerable. Connecting this deep feeling to a need is also another stage of vulnerability. Sharing your needs and values is likely not something that you often do. By sharing these things at one time is sure to make you feel very vulnerable. These two things are both ways of expressing yourself authentically. Therefore, you are practicing honest self-expression. By deciding to be vulnerable even though it is hard and uncomfortable, this inspires compassion in others for a few reasons.

The first reason is that they can see you deciding to be vulnerable and open with them about your feelings. Everyone can relate to how difficult this is, which makes them feel empathy or compassion for you in this situation. Second, because you are expressing a need and know that this is a difficult thing to do, they will also feel empathy or compassion for this need, as being vulnerable shows them that this is important to you. Empathetic and nonviolent communication comes down to recognizing and acknowledging common humanity among yourself and others.

The Benefits of Having and Showing Empathy

When brought into every aspect of a person's life, empathy can have powerful effects on their relationships and life in a general sense. Empathy has the power to do all of the following and more,

- **Heal You and Others**

Empathy has the power to heal. The reason for this is because, to heal, we need other people. To have other people remain there for us in the toughest of times, they need empathy. When they have empathy, they can understand what we are going through, what we may need, and what they can do for us.

Empathy also helps to heal by bridging gaps through creating understanding. When a conflict of any sort occurs, there needs to be healing after resolving this conflict, mostly if the dispute involved angry words or hurt feelings. After a conflict of this sort, you must use empathy to bridge the gap between the parties involved. They must reach a mutual understanding to heal, and empathy is what allows this to happen.

- **Calm the Mind**

Empathy can calm the mind. Empathy does this because it allows a person to practice gratitude and brings them into the present moment. Empathy and meditation are closely linked. Meditation brings about feelings of calm and awareness, while empathy does quite the same.

- **Increase Intimacy**

Finally, empathy can break the silence. Empathy can lead to intimacy and connection, which also leads to dialogue among people. It is challenging to be open and vulnerable with people, but if you know that you share mutual empathy, you will understand that they will not judge you and be safely open and vulnerable. Understanding this helps people who have a hard time opening up and who don't readily speak their feelings or share their thoughts.

- **Strengthen Relationships**

Empathy also has the power to strengthen relationships. Empathy allows relationships to grow and promotes intimacy among people, even if only in a platonic way. By having empathy, it creates a closeness because of the understanding it brings about someone else. When you can understand another person, this strengthens your bond.

If you have a friend that you are extremely close with, think of what you would feel if they came to you crying. How would you feel if they told you that they were going through something tough? You would likely share their feelings with them even if you were not going through it yourself. This example shows empathy at work. Here is an example of what makes your bond so strong and makes you feel close to this person.

Imagine if this type of empathy existed among people who had had their differences. Or people who just met. Or two people who were arguing over a parking spot. Empathy in these situations would strengthen their connection even if it were the first time they met.

There are many different types of relationships that a person has at one time in their life. We define empathy in relationships as understanding within the heart, which allows us to see the other person's beauty. Empathy is beneficial in every type of relationship. Below are all of these different types of relationships ordered from most intimate to least intimate.

- Romantic
- Familial
- Friend
- Colleague
- Teacher/ Education
- Acquaintance
- Unknown

These relationships are all different, but they all have in common that they all involve empathy to make or keep them strong.

- A Romantic Partner

A romantic relationship will involve empathy- this goes without saying. The two people involved in a romantic relationship are tight on an emotional level, so the presence of empathy is a given. If your romantic partner comes home after a bad day, you can likely feel their tiredness and stress even if you had an alright day. This kind of connection between two people comes from intimacy, and with that comes empathy.

Remember that the definition of empathy in relationships is the following; An understanding within the heart that allows us to see the beauty in the other person. This definition explains why you see the beauty in the other person in a romantic relationship no matter what they are doing- even if they have just finished at the gym and are extremely sweaty.

Using empathy in your communication with your partner shows them that you are listening to them, value their needs, and understand their feelings. Communicating like this promotes trust, feelings of security, and sensitivity. A healthy relationship needs good communication, so using empathetic communication is so important in a romantic relationship. It is necessary and important to express your needs clearly to your partner to avoid resentment or miscommunications.

- A Familial Relationship

A familial relationship is not always intimate, but in many cases, it is the next most intimate after a romantic relationship. With familial relationships, there is an ever-present understanding that you have been together through everything and have grown up together, seeing each other in every situation, which makes this kind of relationship so intimate. This relationship always involves empathy as a family that is forever and always there for you.

Because of this bond, the ways that family members communicate with each other are important, especially in front of children who are still learning, growing, and developing. The important thing to teach here is that empathy and compassion come before behavior management, even if there are feelings of frustration or disappointment. It is okay to feel disappointed in someone or frustrated with their behavior, but it is important to show them that you are still empathetic and compassionate toward them regardless. This example illustrates a key difference between ineffective and effective communication, where ineffective communication often involves the use of anger and raised voices in times of frustration.

The way that effective communication views problem solving is also extremely important when it comes to familial relationships. By modeling for your family members that problem-solving and conflict resolution involves satisfaction for everyone, you show them that they do not have to give up their needs and values to resolve a situation. Provided they are needs included in the hierarchy of needs and not needs, such as "I need that chocolate bar," but this is what we teach when modeling this problem-solving type.

- A Friend

In many cases, a close friendship is the next most intimate relationship after a romantic one, so familial and friend relationships can be interchangeable in terms of their positioning on this list. With a very close friendship, you will feel closely linked to that person with your emotions, and you have likely gone through many of the same things at the same time. This bond leads to a mutual understanding and an ability to understand each other on a deep emotional level.

- A Colleague

A colleague relationship is not the most intimate of relationships, but it is one where empathy can still prove very helpful. In a colleague relationship, you often are required to complete tasks together, and many situations could turn into some type of conflict since it involves a lot of time and stress. In many cases, your colleagues are people you see every day, and this develops a closeness that is different from many other relationships. Even if you are not in the type of relationship with your colleagues that involves sharing your deepest fears and dreams, you can still share your needs and feelings to reach a mutual understanding involving empathy. This understanding will lead to a better working relationship and a more comfortable work environment for you, where you get your needs met, and you feel empathy from others.

Using nonviolent communication and empathy among colleagues will keep the workplace people-focused. Too often, workplaces become focused on numbers and results and rules and deadlines. Using nonviolent communication in the workplace, you can remind everyone that there are still human feelings and needs present behind all of the numbers and targets. Often, even the management within a workplace uses violent communication to motivate and push their staff members. This type of motivation is what we are so used to being exposed to. However, it leads to stressful work environments and competition among colleagues. This type of communication is not effective for long-term motivation as people eventually become resentful and tired of being seen as another producer.

- A Teacher/ Education

Education is a place where the forms of communication used are very important in developing the learning people. In schools for children, they learn much more than just how to count and write; they also learn necessary life skills and interpersonal skills. Part of this is learning how to communicate effectively. It is for this reason that using empathetic communication or nonviolent communication in schools is so important. Nonviolent communication for kids allows them to learn in a judgment-free and shame-free environment, which is essential to their development as mentally healthy adults with a healthy self-esteem level.

Kids are communicated to most often in the school system by threatening the "bad" and rewarding the "good." This type of communication is one of the facets of violent (or ineffective) communication. It is a method of controlling outcomes to get what one wants out of people. By having this modeled for children, they learn that the way they can get what they want as an adult is through violent communication, including threats, rewards, and the absence of empathy or compassion.

Using empathy and nonviolent communication in the classroom promotes feelings of safety, trust, interpersonal bonds, collaboration, learning, and acceptance. An environment like this is ideal for kids, as they need to learn and grow to their full potential.

- An Acquaintance

With an acquaintance, you may not think that you would need to feel any empathy towards them. However, in many cases, your acquaintances are responsible for helping you with things or are people you pass daily, and exercising empathy here will be a nice thing for both of you. If you can understand them and understand, there is one more person in the world who you can say you have a positive relationship with. That is a greatly positive thing.

- An Unknown Person

While this may seem like the last relationship in which empathy would be beneficial or required, it is quite helpful for you and the person you don't know if you share mutual empathy. Mutual empathy is beneficial here because this person may be someone who you pass on the street, someone who works at the coffee shop you went to, or someone who is in the parking lot looking for a spot to park at the same time as you. In any of these cases, approaching the situation with empathy will help you have these small interactions throughout your day without conflict or strife, but with understanding and a pleasant feeling.

- **Improve Your Relationship With Yourself (Self-Empathy)**

Another type of empathy is empathy with and for oneself. You are often the person you forget when talking about how you choose to speak to someone and solve problems. We must not forget that you are as much deserving of your love, kindness, and empathy as anyone else is. You are usually your own worst critic. The way that you assume everyone else is thinking about you is much harsher than any way anyone has ever thought about you other than yourself.

We define self-empathy as a compassionate, deep awareness of your own inner experience. You must meet this awareness of your inner experience with self-empathy. You may be aware of your inner experience and approach it with judgmental and shame-filled thoughts and words. Doing this is not practicing empathy for yourself.

Often, the way that you talk to yourself is the way that you will talk to others. By changing how you talk to other people, you are also showing yourself that you should talk to yourself in this way. By showing empathy to yourself in the same way that you do the most important people in your life, you are more likely to experience good mental health, a lower risk of depression, and a greater self-satisfaction level. You are also better able to forgive yourself for things that you deem to be negative or bad decisions, which allows you to move forward without bringing with you all of the things you feel you have failed at.

CHAPTER 9
Increasing Your Level Of Emotional Intelligence Part 4- Self-Regulation

In this chapter, we will take a closer look at how to conduct yourself in times of anger or intense emotion so that you can begin to improve your emotional intelligence through self-regulation. We will begin by revisiting the topic of self-regulation before looking at some strategies that will help you improve it.

Self-Regulation

Whether you are feeling angry or just in a conflict with another person, it is important to know how to conduct yourself maturely and effectively. Regulating yourself will allow you to get the most out of the interaction without causing undue damage to your mental health or relationships. Increasing your emotional intelligence level requires you to work on your ability to regulate your emotions and control them when need-be.

Controlling and Managing Your Emotions

It is very important to learn how to control and manage your emotions. Later on in this chapter, I will present you with several anger management techniques that will help you when you are feeling angry, and all you want to do is act out in anger. Suppose you tend to act on your feelings of anger with aggression, verbal outbursts, or even physical violence. In that case, these techniques will prove quite useful in your journey of finding effective anger management. The skill of self-regulation will save your relationships and prevent you from acting out in ways that will harm your life.

How to Manage and Control Your Emotions

Throughout the remainder of this chapter, we will look at some strategies that will help you self-regulate and control your emotions. If you struggle with this, take extra time to read through this chapter and practice the techniques outlined the next time you feel emotion taking over you.

What Not To Do

The first step in knowing how to do something is knowing how *not* to do it. Therefore, to begin, we will look at how not to conduct yourself when you feel the anger coming on.

- Blame the Other Person

Often, blaming is what people do when they are afraid of looking bad or being blamed for something. Blaming the other person leads to a circular blaming game where everyone is blaming somebody, and the entire situation becomes a game of passing the blame like a hot potato. It may seem like being the one person who doesn't take part in this game will make you look guilty, but it doesn't work this way. You will be open and vulnerable by opting out of the game and expressing yourself using effective communication strategies without inserting yourself into a losing game.

- Threaten

Threatening is another way that you do not want to conduct yourself. By threatening, people will often then write off the conversation because they feel like you are pushing them into a corner. You don't want to make someone feel like this if you hope to get some sort of resolution from the interaction.

- Guilt-Tripping

Guilt-tripping is another way that people often try to get a specific outcome from an interaction. Guilt-tripping leaves the other person feeling terrible about themselves and will leave you feeling negative about yourself as well. Guilt-tripping is not an effective way to resolve a situation, leading to resentment and stored anger.

- Yelling

Yelling may feel like the way to get your point across, but when you are yelling at people, they often shut down and stop listening, which then has the opposite effect that you wanted. Raising your voice is inevitable sometimes, but what matters is the intent behind it. If you are doing it to force the person to see your perspective or yelling over them to listen to you, this will not prove effective in resolving any sort of conflict. People also will feel like you are attacking them when they are being yelled at, causing them to shut down, and the chance of resolution becomes zero.

- Refuse to Take Responsibility

Finally, when people refuse to take responsibility for their anger and the wat they acted out in anger, they often resort to blaming others for their decisions or shortcomings, failing to speak up when necessary, and complaining about situations, events, and the decisions of others.

What To Do

- Assume Responsibility

The first thing that you want to do when conducting yourself maturely and effectively is assuming responsibility. Assuming responsibility means taking control of the part you play in a situation. It also means accepting the fact that you made the decisions you made, including any consequences that came with it.

Assuming responsibility is often hard to do, especially when assuming responsibility may mean looking bad in front of your boss or accepting that you made the decision, which caused something negative to happen as a result. However, assuming responsibility brings you the respect of the people around you and allows you to live truthfully and genuinely. By doing this, you are transparent with others, which is a very respectable quality—having this quality will lead others to trust you and to thank you for your honesty. They will remember this characteristic that you possess, which will help you in many areas of your life. Doing this also goes for yourself. When something happens, that may not be your desired outcome, accepting that you made the decision that led to it but moving on from it and not blaming yourself or guilt-tripping yourself will help you learn from your mistakes. This example shows how you can take responsibility for your decisions.

If you are unsure how to tell whether you are taking responsibility for your actions or how to do so in the future, one of the best ways to do this is to recognize that you have choices. Many times, our reasoning for things is that "I had no choice." We all know that this could not be farther from the truth. Here is a narrative that we use when we do not want to take responsibility for our actions or decisions, as it makes us feel better to think that we had no other option. The reality is that we always have a choice, and we always have options. The sooner you recognize this, the better off you will be in life, and the sooner you will be assuming responsibility. By understanding that you always have a choice and that this choice is yours to make, you live authentically.

- Learn from Your Mistakes

Once you assume responsibility, you can then learn from your mistakes. Only then can you learn from your mistakes, and not before. If you do not accept responsibility for your decisions or choices, you will not ever feel like you have made a mistake.

Assuming responsibility comes with standing by the decisions you made, which, in hindsight, may not have been the ones that you would make again. Accepting your decisions is what sets those who assume responsibility apart from those who do not. Stand by your decisions, even when they don't lead to ideal outcomes, and decide to learn from your mistakes. Without taking responsibility, you will never learn from your mistakes; you need to recognize that you made a mistake to learn from it. You may be wondering what learning from your mistakes looks like in practice. I will walk you through a step-by-step process that will help you to better understand this below.

Step 1: Recognize the Existence of a Mistake

As I mentioned, the first step in learning from your mistakes recognizes that you made one. Once you do this, you are ready to let it teach you a lesson and make you a better person. Learning this lesson may be the most difficult step, but it is the most important.

Step 2: Recognize the Decision or Choice that Leads to it.

Once you have recognized a mistake, you can work backward to determine what choice or decision led to the mistake. Many times, multiple decisions lead up to an event or occurrence, so pinpointing, which resulted in the mistake, will help you learn from it.

Step 3: Recognize the Thought Process that Leads to it.

Once you have pinpointed the decision that leads to a mistake, think back on your thought process when making that choice or decision. Once you do this, you can see the point where you may have made an error in judgment or where you can now see the decision more clearly. By going back to the thought process, you can intervene at the exact spot where you would change the next time when faced with a similar decision. Once you determine the point where you would make a different choice along the decision-making process, you can then see how every thought or choice after that would be different. Doing this can lead you to see what final decision this would have resulted in.

Step 4: Think About your Ideal Result

Thinking about what you hoped for in terms of an ideal result can help you in that you will work backward and determine what sequence of decisions or thought processes would have led to this ideal result. It is important to recognize that sometimes the results are out of your hands and that you can only do so much to try to make a certain result happen. By recognizing this, you can prepare as best you can for this result, but you won't beat yourself up if factors that are genuinely out of your control determine the result. For example, if you have an audition coming up and choose a song to perform. You can do everything you can to decide which song you will choose and prepare for the audition, but at the end of the day, the choice is out of your hands. Suppose the audition does not go well, and this is due to your song choice. In that case, you can use the steps above to determine where you went wrong in your decision-making process and what you would change the next time. Still, you must also recognize that even if you made these changes next time, the final result is due to others' decision-making.

Step 5: Plan for Next Time

When you are looking ahead to the next time you will make a similar decision, think about your goals in terms of the situation. Planning will help you to make the best choices you can along the way.

Step 6: Repeat

If the situation (or a similar one) occurs again and you still do not get a result that you want, begin again in the process of learning from your mistakes. There is no limit to the number of times you can learn from your mistakes, and the more you do so, the better off you will be in your life.

Every person has made many mistakes, but what is important is not the number of mistakes you have made. What is important is how much you take away from these situations to help you in later scenarios and situations. If you are constantly making mistakes and learning from them, you will be much better off and closer to achieving your goals than

a person who makes few mistakes but never takes responsibility for the ones they do make. Remember this as you go through your life, as it is important not only with anger management but also in every life area.
- Practice Anger Management Techniques
  - Counting

When you feel the anger inside you that makes your blood boil, count up to ten or fifty, depending on your level of anger. If you are furious, make it 100. This technique helps give you time to calm yourself physically. Your heart rate will slow down to a normal level, and your adrenaline responses will subside as well. Taking a step back allows you to pause, breathe, and think more clearly.
- Breathing

When you are angry, your breathing becomes shallow and short. When you feel angry, focus on your breathing by slowing it down and making yourself take long and deep breaths. Inhale through your nose and exhale through your mouth. Focusing on your breathing helps you calm yourself and gives your brain the oxygen it needs to think clearly.
- Saying a Mantra

Having a mantra may seem a little airy-fairy if you are not usually one to use this type of thing, but it proves quite helpful in times of intense emotion. A mantra is a word or a phrase designed for you to repeat, which helps you concentrate on meditation. In day to day life, though, it helps bring your consciousness back to the moment, just like meditation does. Your mantra can be anything, such as "relax," "you're safe," or anything that helps you to calm yourself at the moment. Choose a mantra in a moment of calm and quiet, so it is in the back of your mind when you need it in a moment of anger.
- Stretching

Stretching is a good practice for intense anger moments because it helps to bring you back down to earth. It reconnects you with your body and your muscles, which will help bring you to the moment and help with your blood flow. Any stretches are good; neck rolls, leg stretches, or shoulder rolls are great.
- Visualizing

Visualizing is a great tool for when it is difficult to control your anger. When a person is visualizing, their conscious mind is actively aware that their visualizing is not real but that they are producing it via imagination. Despite this, a person's subconscious can't identify the difference between what a person imagines and what they are doing. In other words, a person's inner mind isn't able to distinguish the difference between real life, an imagined future, or a memory. Rather, the mind is under the impression that everything a person sees is real. Visualization proves through numerous brain scans that scientists have conducted over the years. They discovered no difference in brain activity when someone is observing something in the real world compared to when a person is visualizing.

All of this evidence is extremely important because it points to the theory that by using visualization, people can develop skills that are completely new to them and be able to reprogram and rewire their mind without the requirement of performing those actions physically. For example, the person can imagine their ideal relaxing scenario without having to get themselves there physically.

Using the technique of calming oneself in a person's mind can help them effectively rewire their brain to build new patterns, habits, and behaviors. Rewiring makes completing these tasks in the real world far less difficult. For example, imagining a relaxing scenario when you feel anger coming on will eventually make it easier for your brain and body to relax without using visualization. Due to this, you will feel much calmer when you practice relaxation in times of anger.

To begin practicing this, go somewhere quiet and get comfortable. Close your eyes and visualize your ideal relaxing scene. Imagine you are there. Imagine the sights, smells, sounds, and feelings that you would be experiencing. By doing this, you are tricking your brain into thinking you are in this scene, which will bring you feelings of relaxation, joy, and comfort.

- Pausing

If you are having an outburst of yelling out everything that you would not have said had you not been so angry, make yourself stop talking. Glue your lips together, and do not allow yourself to open them for a few minutes. This time where you cannot allow yourself to spit out a slew of words that you do not mean will give you some time to think before you decide what you want to say or do.

- Exercising

Exercise does great things for your body, especially in times of intense anger. The positive feelings of "runner's high" that you get after doing exercise will help to dispel some of your anger. Also, putting your anger into the gym will help you harness and take your anger out healthy.

Getting active is a great solution when you have the time. Often, when people feel angry, they likely do not want to get up and do something physical. However, exercising is a great way to relieve stress and anger. You don't have to spend hours at the gym to reap the benefits; you can simply do a light exercise. One way to do this is to go for a quick walk to allow your brain to release the endorphins that make you feel good. People get the most benefit from exercise if they do it for at least 30 minutes per day. Small exercise activities will add up over a day. Here are some suggestions that you can try to incorporate into your schedule:

- Play an active game with your family/friends (e.g., ping pong, Wii)
- Find an exercise partner and hold each other accountable.

- Parking your car as far as you can and get yourself to walk to wherever you're going
- Walk to do your errands instead of driving.
- If you have a dog, take him/her out for a walk.
- Play some music and dance around
  - Writing

There are likely many things you want to say, but you know it will end up doing more harm than good, especially if you say them in a time of anger. Write these things down. This way, you are still expressing yourself and your anger, but you are not hurting anyone or your relationships by doing so. Writing helps you process your emotions and helps you examine them from afar to decide the best course of action.

- Ranting

Ranting to someone who is not involved in the situation can help you express yourself without offending someone involved and risking damaging your relationship. Healthy ranting to a third party helps allow you to express yourself and process the situation and your feelings about it.

- Laughing

Laughing can help to diffuse your anger. Laughing is strong medicine, so making yourself laugh when feeling intense feelings of anger can help you to relax a little and take a step back. Watching a funny show, talking to a friend who makes you laugh, or scrolling the internet for funny content are all ways of doing this.

- Practicing Relaxation

The most effective ways of controlling anger involve relaxation. If you feel like you are getting angry too often, and your level of anger is not as much the problem as the rate at which it recurs, practicing relaxation techniques will prove quite useful.

A quick and easy relaxation technique is to remind yourself to relax. Simply remembering that this is the goal will help you stop and think about the techniques stored in the back of your mind, giving you time to recall them. Relaxing will not only help you relax but will distract you from your anger momentarily. Then, when you remember it, you may not feel that it is as intense as you first thought.

When anger takes over your body, it can be difficult to think clearly or rationally, and it is often without thought that we act. You can try several techniques to ensure that you don't lash out in anger when you are feeling sad.

- Relaxing Using Mindfulness

Mindfulness is a type of mental training practice that involves focusing your mind on your thoughts and sensations in the present moment. You will focus on your current emotions, physical sensations, and passing thoughts. Mindfulness usually involves breathing practice, mental imagery, awareness of your mind and body, and muscle and body relaxation. Using mindfulness can be beneficial in anger management as it will help you connect to your body and mind, which will allow you to control your anger.

The most popular reason people decide to learn meditation is to achieve mindfulness to combat mental obstacles. If you live a very fast-paced and stressful life, mindfulness and meditation can help you manage your thoughts and emotions to bring you more peace. Many doctors who specialize in mental health have begun to study and even practice meditation and mindfulness techniques to promote a healthier brain and mind.

You can achieve mindfulness through the use of meditation. What exactly does this entail? There is a famous quote said by Pema Chodron: "MeditationMeditation is a process of lightening up, of trusting the basic goodness of what we have and who we are, and of realizing that any wisdom that exists, exists in what we already have. We can lead our life to become more awake to who we are and what we're doing rather than trying to improve or change or get rid of who we are or what we're doing. The key is to wake up, to become more alert, more interested, and curious about ourselves."

To get into a state of mindfulness involves getting quiet and observing, without judgment, everything that occurs within your body. Most of the time, we are mindlessly moving through the world, acting without thought. By functioning mindlessly, you train your mind to feel more satisfaction when you choose tasks that produce instant gratification rather than tasks that you should be doing to achieve your goal. When it comes to anger management, this comes in the form of acting out in anger instead of using the techniques you have learned. One way to avoid this is by using mindfulness.

- Using Mindfulness To Self-Regulate

There are many ways that a person can practice mindfulness to manage their anger. You could simply just sit quietly for five minutes and concentrate on the environment around you and pay attention to what thoughts are going through your mind as you are observing. Self-regulation will help you to look at your anger and allow it to dissipate. If you are a beginner at mindfulness, consider taking meditation classes to get a good foundation. As a beginner, try to practice mindfulness via guided sessions. Once you get a good grip on it, you can begin to just start practicing mindfulness everywhere you go by using some of the techniques you've learned.

Mindfulness and meditation go hand in hand. Meditation increases mindfulness while mindfulness improves and deepens meditation. Meditation is a practice, while mindfulness is a state of being.

Another example of mindfulness practice is the following. Get quiet and sit with yourself in silence. Close your eyes. You must let your thoughts drift by, noticing but not judging them. Pay attention to sensations in your body; is there tightness or tension anywhere? Notice the feeling of your chest rising and falling with each breath, the weight of your body on the chair/ bed you are in. Notice also your emotions and feelings. By doing this repeatedly, you will be able to eventually focus on your body with less and less distracting thoughts. When your thoughts start to distract you, bring your attention back to your body, and your breathing. Being able to reach a state like this allows you to reconnect with your body from the inside. Approaching your body with a non-judgment mindset will also make it easier for you to change your beliefs about your body or introduce new thoughts and behaviors. Instead of letting your mind spiral with anxious *what-if* thoughts, you will not let them escalate. They will not escalate to the level they normally would because instead of judging yourself and your body and worrying about what is wrong with you, you will approach it as is and without trying to force anything.

By focusing on the body and letting your thoughts enter your consciousness one by one, you can untangle them, resulting in a reduction in stress level. The state of meditation also brings about a state of relaxation and calm. Often, we are running around with a mind full of running thoughts, one after the other. When we take time to sit in silence, breathe, and sort through everything we are thinking and feeling through a non-judgmental lens, it leads to a state of inner peace. This inner peace state makes it much easier for your body to let in and embrace the good feelings and allows your mind to be more open and receptive to them.

CHAPTER 10
Increasing Your Level Of Emotional Intelligence Part 5- Self-Awareness

This chapter is our final chapter of the book, and the final chapter will discuss strategies for increasing your level of emotional intelligence. In this chapter, we will talk about self-awareness and how it will help you increase your emotional intelligence.

What Is Self-Awareness?

Self-awareness is being aware of the 'self' to put it simply. We began to study self-awareness as a psychological study back in 1972. Psychologists concluded that when we focus our attention on our inner selves, we can evaluate and compare our current behavior to the standards and values we hold for ourselves. We become self-conscious and become objective evaluators of our actions.

The Relationship Between Self-Awareness and Emotional Intelligence

As we saw above, Psychologists concluded that self-awareness is the foundation of self-control. Therefore, self-awareness is part of the foundation of Emotional Intelligence as well.

Self-awareness goes way beyond just gaining knowledge about ourselves. Self-awareness focuses on paying attention to our inner state and wellbeing with an open mind and heart. Our mind is exceptional at storing information and memories about how we react to certain situations to form a blueprint of our emotional life. Such information ends up training our mind to react the same way when we encounter similar situations in the future. Being self-aware allows us to be aware of the mind's conditioning and training, which can be the stepping stone to freeing the mind from it.

So, does self-awareness matter? According to psychologists, self-awareness is the cornerstone to achieving emotional intelligence. The ability to monitor and control our thoughts and feelings from minute to minute is important to understanding ourselves more, being comfortable with who we are, and proactively organizing our thoughts, behaviors, and emotions. Additionally, self-aware people act consciously rather than passively and usually have good mental wellbeing and a positive view of life. They also tend to have larger and deeper life experience and are likely to be more compassionate. A scientific study in 2016 studied the parts of self-awareness and the benefits. They found that mindfulness, insight, and self-reflection are all aspects of self-awareness and lead to benefits like; becoming a more accepting person and less emotional burdens. The research also found that self-awareness is a critical trait for people who want to be successful business leaders.

How to Improve Your Level of Self-Awareness

If self-awareness is so important, why are humans not more self-aware? The obvious answer to that is that we do not pay attention to ourselves enough because we cannot observe ourselves from the outside. We are simply not paying enough attention to the things going on inside and outside of us.

- Get Out of Autopilot Mode

Often in our lives, we are on "auto-pilot mode," which means that we are not paying attention to what we are doing, how we are feeling, or what we are saying to others. We let our minds wander elsewhere rather than being in the moment, leading to complete unawareness of how we conduct ourselves.

Constant mind-wandering is a symptom of lacking self-awareness. Mind-wandering affects our ability to have a good and accurate understanding of ourselves. As a result of this, we tend to believe what our inner voice says to us about the kind of person we are. For example, if we had a strong belief that we are loyal friends, we are more likely to interpret events (even if we made a mistake) as an anomaly of our identity as a "loyal friend." This pre-existing belief of ourselves may influence how we handle the aftermath of situations. For example, if we accidentally forgot about a dinner date with a friend, you may brush it off and tell yourself that it is a one-off since you normally perceive yourself as a "loyal friend."

So, what can we do to improve this?

Sometimes we would rather distract ourselves and cover up our emotions and our truth than to feel them or to face them head-on. In this case, our brain may occupy us or run on autopilot to distract us from facing the truth. When we have a quiet minute where these feelings or thoughts would creep into our minds, we cover them up or push them away by occupying ourselves with something else and convincing ourselves that we are "too busy" to acknowledge our feelings.

Distracting yourself can be a problem if this reoccurs and begins to impact your level of emotional intelligence. If there is something that you think you may be avoiding dealing with or thinking about, or if you tend to be very uncomfortable with feelings of unrest, you may be experiencing this type of distraction and autopilot living.

The first step to combatting this is to recognize this pattern. Recognizing your struggles will also help you to have a better relationship with your mind. Understanding how your mind works will help you to better take care of it. You will be able to recognize your feelings and what they could be caused by, and then treat them in a way that will help it to feel better. By improving your relationship with your mind by listening to it, you will begin to give it the attention and care that it needs. Paying closer attention will, in turn, lead to better cognitive functioning, control over impulses, and decision-making, to name a few. Changing this will help overall in your relationships and your life as a whole. By facing this struggle head-on, you can begin to become more self-aware.

- Challenge Your Limiting Beliefs And Negative Self-Talk

We all have an inner voice that is undoubtedly at work in your mind day in and day out. This voice can benefit you, but much of the time, it is working against you. Also, we all hold beliefs- about the world, ourselves, life, and so on. These beliefs can either help us move forward in our lives positively or hold us back by keeping us focused on the negative, on things that we cannot control, and the problems in our lives. A *limiting belief* is something that we believe informs our actions and behaviors. These actions and behaviors coincide with our belief, which, in turn, holds us back or limits us in some way.

For example, if you believe that other people are to blame for your unhappiness, this would limit belief. By believing this, you will see your negative internal state of mind due to other people's actions and shortcomings. Beliefs such as this can keep you stuck in a very dark and negative place until you realize that this belief is not, in fact, true. By understanding and learning that you are the only person responsible for your internal state, you can begin to take it into your own hands and change it, no longer limiting yourself. This kind of limiting belief, which is not rooted in truth, will lead you away from true self-awareness and toward a life full of limitations and a low level of emotional intelligence.

Negative self-talk goes hand-in-hand with limiting beliefs, as it also is something that goes on without your knowledge most of the time, likely because you are so used to having negative self-talk running in the background of your mind all day long. Your negative self-talk comes from something called your inner critic.

Your inner critic lives in a black and white world, a world with very little room for the grey area, and where failure is the worst possible outcome of every scenario. Your inner critic shares words with you, such as, "You should just give up" Or "What makes you think you'll succeed?" Instead of creating an open space that allows for mistakes, growth, and development, your inner critic causes you to question your worth. Questioning your worth makes it difficult for you to have the positive, growth mindset needed to complete tasks and go after things that may be difficult to achieve. For some people, their inner critic is reminiscent of a voice from their past- it could be their mother, father, or person who bullied them. For others, it could simply be their voice criticizing them for everything they do. Sometimes, if a person makes an offhand comment at you, this could lead you to absorb it so deeply that the words they said become a part of your identity.

When we continue to judge ourselves harshly (with the help of our negative inner voice), we may think that we are making progress in getting closer to change or improving our flaws. In reality, we are only reinforcing the feelings of unworthiness that lie deep within which end up holding us back. In our world today, it is a cultural norm to believe that self-criticism will bring motivation to achieving goals and avoiding procrastination. This type of self-criticism functions under the false belief that when a person realizes that their actions or performance isn't good enough, they'll want to change.

The inner critic is also guilty for giving us a sense of control, but not over the correct things. We also use our judgmental thoughts to cope with emotions such as shame, fear, and things that we do not understand. Over time, these comments made by yourself or other people manifest inside you and eventually become your own unique "inner critic." To put it in its simplest form, your inner critic is the persistent negative self-talk that keeps you stuck in the same place (mentally, emotionally, and physically) for much too long.

When people have developed unhelpful thinking processes, it is hard to benefit their future selves because their thoughts create negative emotions that drive away motivation. Some people argue that by simply increasing your willpower, thus overcoming the need for instant gratification, you will fix your situation. This belief, however, is not an effective solution for long-lasting change. In this section, we will look at a variety of ways that you can begin to combat those limiting beliefs and the negative self-talk that goes on in your mind.

- Remind Yourself To Be Positive

As we learned, we build bad habits over many years, and no amount of willpower can handle overcoming that many bad habits in a person's life. Rewiring your brain to minimize the amount of negativity you feel in the first place is a much more efficient method to approach this problem.

- Catch Yourself Thinking According To Your Limiting Beliefs

Often, if the person had just paid attention to their thought process, they would be able to catch themselves before their mind automatically spiraled to a place of complete de-motivation. By catching yourself before you get there, you can prevent yourself from falling into your negative thought patterns, limiting you and holding you back.

- Show Yourself Evidence Against Your Limiting Belief

Showing yourself evidence that supports or doesn't support the thoughts that are on your mind will help you to change your limiting beliefs. Showing yourself evidence can cancel out those negative thinking styles and give yourself the confidence and motivation to overcome any situation.

If a person remains in the mindset that, "Oh I'm going to fail and embarrass myself anyway, so why prepare?" Then the majority of the time, people of this mindset will choose to not prepare, thus leading to a feeling of failure when they inevitably do not come prepared for success. This feeling of failure further solidifies their limiting belief.

When your inner critic begins to tell you that you can't do a certain thing, or you're not good enough, or you're not worthy enough, simply find evidence within your past life experiences that challenge or discount this belief. Prove your inner critic wrong and show them why holding you back is only going to do more harm than if you failed whatever task you were planning to do. The more you tell your inner critic this, the more they will learn to listen to you and help you in another way that is not just preventing you from doing things.

- Ask For Support From Your Inner Critic

If your inner-critic is telling you that you will embarrass yourself and everyone will laugh at you, you can prove it wrong by using evidence-based arguments. You can also negotiate with it to let you try it out, and then ask for its support by saying, "This is a difficult challenge for me, and I want to overcome it. I need you to be by my side, regardless of the outcome." Remember, your inner critic is just another version of yourself. Be kind to your inner critic, even if it's not kind to you. Show yourself kindness- this is very important in your case.

- Negotiate With Your Limiting Beliefs To Change Them

When you can notice these voices and statements that are going on in your brain according to your limiting beliefs, you can then simply acknowledge them and begin to negotiate with your inner critic. Let them know that you thank them for looking out for you, but you are confident in your ability to make decisions for yourself. You can let them know that even though you may fail and feel embarrassed, it is still better than a lifetime of holding back. Since your inner critic is a part of you, after all, it can listen to reason as long as you allow yourself to reason with your mind.

- Surround Yourself With Positive People

Surrounding yourself with people that can encourage you and foster positivity will also change your inner-critic opinion. Often, hearing positive compliments from other people holds a heavier weight in the eyes of your inner-critic compared to you telling your inner-critic the same thing. Try spending time with people who support your goals and the changes you are looking to make in your life. It will make your journey a little bit easier.

CONCLUSION

Thank you for taking the time to read this book; I hope you found the information helpful! I wrote this book to help you accomplish your goals of changing your life. The hope is that this book will increase your level of emotional intelligence (or EI) and enhance your experience as a whole.

Upon reading this book and taking time to let the concepts settle in your mind, I hope you will find that your life changes in many ways! By increasing your level of emotional intelligence, you will find that your relationships grow stronger and more intimate, your workplace performance and relationships increase, and that your life as a whole becomes more enriched. You will thank yourself for reading this book for years to come.

Due to our society's nature, many people operate on an "auto-pilot" mode throughout their day, never stopping to think about their lives or actions. By reading this book, you take a step back and evaluate yourself, which is the first step to making change.

This book will teach you how to live a healthier and more fulfilling life without ever having to think too much about it.
It is not easy to change your life, especially if you have been living a certain way for a long time. After reading this book, I hope that you are well-equipped to begin making changes in your life, no matter how small. The key here will be practice, as improving emotional intelligence does not happen overnight. It is proven to improve with some practice, and you will need to stick with it to see lasting changes. Remember, everyone's perception of reality is different. You can start small by asking others for their opinion and try to understand what they are feeling, while also getting in touch with and communicating your feelings.
With your new knowledge of everything to do with emotional intelligence and how to improve it, what are the next steps? The answer is consistency!
Now that you have finished reading this book, please share it with your friends and family. Sharing this book will increase our societies' emotional intelligence as a whole and a better overall world.

DESCRIPTION

Are you a person that often understands how others are feeling? Do you understand your own emotions? Or are you someone that is always confused as to how other people feel? Do you have trouble looking at something from another person's point of view? Do you want to change your life, but you are unsure of where to begin? If you feel like you could use help in any of these areas, this book is for you!

Within the pages of this book, you will find the following topics, among others;

- What is Emotional Intelligence (EI)?
- Attributes of people with low Emotional intelligence
- Attributes of people with high Emotional intelligence
- How can Emotional Intelligence benefit you?
- The areas of your life that will help
- Why should you increase your level of Emotional Intelligence?
- The benefits of high EI in the workplace
- The benefits of high EI in relationships
- How to increase your Emotional Intelligence
- Strategies for increasing your EI
- Controlling and managing your emotions
- The benefits of having and showing empathy
- Reflecting on and understanding your emotions
- How to begin understanding your emotions
- The importance of maintaining high EI
- How to maintain a high level of EI

The above topics will not only provide you with many tips and methods for improving your emotional intelligence. They will also give you a strong basic understanding of what emotional intelligence is and how it functions. By understanding what it entails, you will be more invested in the process, which will prevent you from giving up early.

This book is effective because it teaches you how to employ realistic and useful habits and techniques that anyone can use to increase their emotional intelligence. The concepts within this book are easy to understand and apply as long as they keep an open mind and a learning mindset. An open mind is one that can begin to understand anything you like. The opportunities are endless for those who keep it open. This is the first thing that you will learn in this book. Once you understand this concept, we will begin to look into deeper and more complex ideas surrounding emotional intelligence.

Upon reading this book, you will find that your life changes in many ways! By increasing your level of emotional intelligence, you will find that your relationships grow stronger and more intimate, your workplace performance and relationships increase, and that your life as a whole becomes more enriched. You will thank yourself for reading this book for years to come.

The first step you need to take in growing your emotional intelligence is learning more about it. The best way to do this is to read a book that can take you from beginning to end, packed full of concepts and information, which you have now done. First of all, I'd like to congratulate you on having the self-discipline to stick with something and finishing this book. You have already proven your ability that you do have self-discipline; you just need to learn to apply it in other areas of our life. With all this new information that you just learned, what's next for you?

This book not only gives you the information that you need to decide that you need to make a change in your life, but it also contains a wealth of solutions that you can begin to put into practice immediately for you to make those lasting changes.

HOW TO ANALYZE PEOPLE

Read Human Behaviors, Learn Body Language, And Analyze Nonverbal Communication Using Emotional Intelligence

Samantha Scott

© Copyright 2020 by Samantha Scott. All right reserved.

The work contained herein has been produced with the intent to provide relevant knowledge and information on the topic on the topic described in the title for entertainment purposes only. While the author has gone to every extent to furnish up to date and true information, no claims can be made as to its accuracy or validity as the author has made no claims to be an expert on this topic. Notwithstanding, the reader is asked to do their own research and consult any subject matter experts they deem necessary to ensure the quality and accuracy of the material presented herein.

This statement is legally binding as deemed by the Committee of Publishers Association and the American Bar Association for the territory of the United States. Other jurisdictions may apply their own legal statutes. Any reproduction, transmission or copying of this material contained in this work without the express written consent of the copyright holder shall be deemed as a copyright violation as per the current legislation in force on the date of publishing and subsequent time thereafter. All additional works derived from this material may be claimed by the holder of this copyright.

The data, depictions, events, descriptions and all other information forthwith are considered to be true, fair and accurate unless the work is expressly described as a work of fiction. Regardless of the nature of this work, the Publisher is exempt from any responsibility of actions taken by the reader in conjunction with this work. The Publisher acknowledges that the reader acts of their own accord and releases the author and Publisher of any responsibility for the observance of tips, advice, counsel, strategies and techniques that may be offered in this volume.

INTRODUCTION

Congratulations on purchasing *How to Analyze People,* and thank you for doing so.

Imagine that you have just encountered a person. You and the other person do not know each other at all. You look at him, and he looks at you, and you seem to have some sort of mutual understanding between the two of you. You walk around him, and he walks around you before you both head off. You then move on about your day without thinking anything of it.

A little bit later, you walk past another person. This person looks at you, and immediately, in your gut, you feel nervous. You can't explain it—you don't know what it is or why you feel that way, but, suddenly, you are afraid—more afraid than you thought you would be. What do you do? How do you approach the situation? You end up trying to beeline it out of the area that you are in. That night, you see something chilling on the news: That same person that you passed nervously was arrested for stealing something.

You don't know how you knew that this person was up to no good, but you did. You don't know how to explain it, but you chose to avoid him rather than heading further down that road, where you very well could have been the one robbed instead. How did you know? Intuition? Guardian angel? Sheer dumb luck?

Nope.

The answer is through body language. Unconsciously, you knew that this person posed a threat due to the body language that he put off. Even if he had approached you with a smile on his face, there is a very good chance that the rest of his body language would not jive. This is not some sort of magic or anything else—it is biology.

We are naturally equipped with a sense of being able to read the body language of others. We understand the importance of being able to read what someone else is doing, what they are thinking, how they choose to behave, and why they do what they do. We have evolved to be able to read the body language of other humans because of the value it brings. When you can look at your tribe and know what the rest of them are thinking or feeling in the state of nature, you can know that ultimately, you need to do something, or ultimately, everything is okay. By being able to look to the body language of other people, we get an instant snapshot of what is going on in their minds, similar to how dogs will read other dogs that they approach. The ability to read body language is not unique to humans—in fact, the vast majority of animals have some degree of body language. Typically, the more social the animal, the more complex the body language becomes as a result. So, what does this mean for you, then?

It means that learning to read body language is one of the best things that you can do for yourself. When you learn to read body language, you are able to begin interacting with people in far more effective manners. When you engage in that sort of body language with other people, you can find yourself becoming far better at understanding the minds of those around you. You can become more capable of understanding intentions as well as being more effective at communicating in general.

Overall, being able to read body language is one of the most important skills that you can learn during the course of your life, and the sooner that you develop it, the better. That is exactly what this book is here for—as you read through this book, you can expect to learn all about what it will take to learn to analyze other people. You will learn why we make it a point to analyze others, how important it becomes to be able to understand the mind of other people by watching the body, and how you can begin to use analyzing others to benefit yourself. From there, it will be time to look at what can be done to understand nonverbal cues and the process of reading people, and then it is time to address the various points to read. We will go over how to read the face, the body, the legs, and feet, and take a look at a few other types of body language as well, such as proxemics and haptics—the usage of distance and touch to help with communication. Then, we will take the time to go over how to use body language—both in reading common clusters of body language and in being able to use it to influence others as well.

As you read, you will learn everything that you will need to get started with reading other people. You will learn about being able to understand the intentions that people have, what they choose to do with themselves, and more, all by reading through this book. Keep in mind that sometimes, being able to read someone else may actually save someone's life. It can really change lives.

You will learn how you can start benefiting yourself and other people through being able to read body language as well. Did you know that sometimes, people do not know what they want, though their body language is screaming it, loud and clear for them? When you learn to appreciate this fact and approach the situation as being able to understand them, you can use that as well. You can help people. You can put them at ease if you need to. You can convince them that they want something when they are a bit iffy on the situation. Ultimately, the best way to ensure that you can put yourself in this position is to learn to read them in the first place, and that is where this book comes in. You will learn these skills that you ought to have. You will ensure that you are in a position that you can better help those around you, and it will be highly compelling for you and for those around you. So, are you ready to become a much better person? Are you ready to see how your own body language matters here? If so, then keep reading… This book is here to teach you to do exactly that.

There are plenty of books on this subject on the market; thanks again for choosing this one! Every effort was made to ensure it is full of as much useful information as possible; please enjoy!

CHAPTER 1
The Purpose Of Analyzing Others

When we think about communication, we almost always consider the idea of talking or writing. We think about words themselves. Communication becomes something that, without words, we do not really consider. After all, how much is really communicated by standing around without making a sound? The truth is—it is incredibly telling.

Communication comes primarily in two different forms. It can be used verbally, meaning with the use of words in various forms, or it can be nonverbal, in which case it is silent and without the need for sounds at all. Nonverbal communication is able to be discerned at a glance toward other people, and it is incredibly valuable. When you can communicate nonverbally, you can communicate in ways that do not require you to hear a single word spoken. You can look at someone and understand so much about them at just a glance.

This is so important when you consider the fact that people are largely social and are driven by their need to interact with each other. Being able to communicate directly with each other becomes one of the most important parts of remaining a society. Think about it—if you cannot communicate, how can you cooperate? If you have on the way to make it clear what you are thinking about or hearing said, how can you possibly make it a point to change up how you choose to engage? Ultimately, being able to address the situations that you are in requires communication, and sometimes, that communication needs to be quiet.

Of course, we also use the ability to analyze others for more than just communication as well. It is used to be able to identify the emotions of other people, which becomes a highly compelling ability to have. It allows you to begin to recognize whether someone else is attempting to deceive you, as well—when you can tell when someone is lying, you can protect yourself from the collateral damage that would come along with it. You can tell if someone has attracted you as well, thanks to recognizing the signs, and you will also be able to identify and understand the thoughts that someone else may have. Finally, when you consider the ability that you gain from being able to analyze the thoughts of other people, you discover that being able to read to other people, you get a package of communication that is undeniably important.

Being able to analyze others can be the difference between being scammed and being able to tell when someone is trying to take advantage of you. Being able to tell when someone else is being threatened or attempting to assert dominance over you is perfect. When you can do this, you know precisely when it is that people need to be addressed. You will be able to see how to cut out the nonsense so you can ensure that you are able to make judgments that are highly supported by information that you already have about something.

Analyzing Others for Identifying Emotions

When it comes to analyzing other people, you can gain all sorts of information that is highly beneficial. Perhaps one of the best parts, however, is being able to analyze others to identify their emotions as you go along the way. This is imperative—when you can see the emotions that other people have, you can then begin to figure out what it is that they do. When it comes to being able to identify the emotions of other people, you find yourself in a position where you can start to interact with them better.

Think about it—when you work together with other people, you have to be in communication with them somehow. It makes sense, then, that you would be able to read the emotional state of that person at any given point in time. If emotions themselves are designed to motivate us into acting in certain situations, when we have other people capable of understanding our motivations as well, we can coordinate far better. Think about it—if you look at your partner and see that he is angry, you can realize that something somewhere is a threat, whether that is your own direct actions or if it is something else. By being able to tell the difference, you should be able to figure out what it is that you can do to help. You can tell if the problem is that you have overstepped or if someone else has instead. By working to figure this out, little by little, you can start to piece together exactly how you need to interact.

Likewise, when you can see the emotional state of someone else, you can help them when they need it. You will be able to help them to work through their problems. Think about how, when you see someone that is sad, you naturally want to help, especially if you know the other person or have some vested interest in their behaviors. This is important to keep in mind—when you are able to do this, you start to empathize more because you are reading their body language.

Analyzing Others to Identify Lying

Another benefit of analyzing people is that you can tell when people are attempting to deceive you. There is very clear body language that can be looked at that determines when you are being deceived, and the sooner that you learn to read it, the better. Think about it—how often do you simply take people at face value when they tell you something? When you work in sensitive fields that involve important sensitive information, such as requiring social security numbers, money, and the like, you will need to ensure that you can tell if they are lying. Think about it—if you are going to sell something to someone and your business requires you to be able to make money through these sales, you want to make sure that you have a client that is not going to be problematic. If you want to ensure that you can better engage with the entire situation, you must ensure that you choose to approach the situation accordingly. This means that you need to be able to tell when someone is deceptive.

Other fields are even more sensitive—if you are a lawyer or an investigator, you will need to be able to tell when someone else is lying. You must make sure that you can see it in the face of the other person so you can ensure that you are getting the whole truth. Think about it—if you are a bankruptcy attorney and you are getting information from your client, you will be submitting that information to the court of law, and you must be as honest as possible, or you risk perjury charges. This means that you need to be disclosing all information as required by law. If your client lies to you, you need to be able to spot it.

This is also important in interpersonal relationships as well—you must be able to tell what is going on with those around you. If you are being asked to help someone or loan something to a friend, you want to know that they are willing to pay it back as agreed. You must be able to see that your friends are honest and truthful and that they are not trying to take you for a ride at your expense. Being able to read when someone is deceiving you has so many benefits in just about every single aspect of your life, and it all begins with being able to see the truth in the matter. It all starts with analyzing people and their body language to get the fullest picture of the situation.

Analyzing Others to Identify Attraction

Analyzing others also matters in the dating scene, believe it or not. When you know what to look for in terms of body language, you can start to spot the people that are attracted or interested in you. Think about it—if you are heading out into the dating scene, you want to know where you have a chance and where you may not. You will be able to see when someone appears to be attracted to you so you can identify whether you have a chance. You will also be able to use this as a sort of metric for whether your date is actually interested in you in the first place.

Would you really want to waste your time on a date with someone that is not interested in you? Would you really want to spend time trying to force a date with someone that does not seem driven to continue? Most people would not—and because of that, you want to be able to tell what is going on with other people in their minds to control how you engage with everyone around you. Ultimately, the more that you go through the effort of doing so, the more that you will realize that being able to read the other person.

CHAPTER 2
Can You Really Understand The Mind By Watching The Body?

Now, you might be doubtful that you can actually understand the mind and what is going on inside of it just by looking at the body, but the truth is, you can tell an awful lot just by taking a look at what other people are doing. This is why you get that gut reaction when someone charges at you to tell their intent. You can tell the difference between whether someone runs toward you happily or angrily all by looking at the body language. This is more than just facial features, too—it is all about everything. Body language is visible in how people move, how they position themselves, what they do with touching other people, how they relate to each other, and more. When it comes to being able to tell how people engage, you can tell so much through paying attention to those little movements and actions.

As you read through this book, you will be guided through understanding this nonverbal communication so you can better read it. You will be able to tell what it is that someone is thinking for one simple reason: The body will almost always betray the mind. Your unconscious thoughts that drive everything are highly visible just by learning to analyze the body itself. Think about it—you can tell from a glance when someone is shy versus when they are simply uninterested in being around other people.

Before we start delving into how to analyze people, let's take a look at the science behind it. Within this chapter, we are going to address the idea of body language as an unconscious manifestation of the thoughts that you have within your own mind. With that approach, you can begin to see what it will take to understand the minds of those around you. You will discover how you can better understand and interpret the thoughts just by virtue of being able to do some backward sleuthing. Through backtracking through the thoughts, you can then begin to recognize what is going on inside the minds of those around you. When you are able to piece together that backtrack, you get to see precisely what is happening inside the minds of the other people. As you learn to understand their minds, you get to also influence them as well. Through being able to influence them as well, you will be able to figure out what you must do with them. You will be able to find ways that you can better assume how you will engage with the other person to grant yourself that added level of control that you were looking for.

The Body Betrays the Mind

When it comes to being able to read the mind, your body will always betray your mind. This is because your body language is primarily controlled by your subconscious mind. The subconscious mind is responsible for your ability to respond and react to the world around you—it is there to help you understand how to engage with the world around you. When you are going about your day, your mind is primarily focused entirely on what you are doing at any given moment. Think about it—you are probably currently focused on how you are reading this book right now. You are not paying attention to the surroundings, at least not consciously. You are not actively listening to other people or what they are talking about. You are not paying attention to the television show that is on in front of you. You are not doing anything but read these words across the page. However, if you were to hear something that was pertinent to you, such as someone saying your name, you would hear it. This is because your unconscious mind is listening to everything in the background. Though you may not be paying attention yourself, your unconscious mind is listening to everything that is going on around you. It is filtering out anything that you need to pay attention to while ignoring everything else. As a result, you will find that ultimately, you can do better—you can respond well to the surroundings because you paid just enough attention.

Your subconscious mind is important when it comes to how you navigate through the world. Think about it—when you go through life with your unconscious mind as your copilot, you are constantly absorbing information from all around you, even if you are not really paying attention to it. This is why something moving in the corner of your eye can catch your attention, or hearing someone call your name will snap you out of whatever you are doing. Your subconscious mind is paying attention, and it will then respond by pushing that particular stimulus to your conscious mind.

This is imperative to understand—when you recognize this, you will see that ultimately, you can better understand the next concept that we are about to discuss, and that is that the subconscious mind is also directly responsible for controlling your body language as well. Your subconscious cannot directly communicate with your conscious mind—but, it can influence how you feel. It can also influence how it reads the body language of other people. As a result, the way that you approach most situations is highly dependent upon your subconscious mind.

Imagine this situation for a moment—you are taking a walk around the park. You don't know anyone that is present there as you are not in your usual neighborhood. You walk along, and suddenly, you feel a sensation of nervousness. You cannot explain it—but you feel concerned about something. As you walk around, you cannot figure out what it is that is bothering you, but it is clear that there is something. You walk around, you think about it, and you cannot identify those feelings of doubt. However, the more that you walk, the more that you feel that way. Eventually, you realize what it is-- it is the fact that there is someone that has been near you at every turn through the park. Something about his body language is setting off that instinct within yourself that you must be cautious around him. You can't explain it, but the feeling is there. As a result, you find yourself paying more attention to him, and he leaves.

Your subconscious is what caught on to the fact that you needed to be more cautious. It warned you that you needed to pay attention at that moment so you would be safe, and it let you know that ultimately, you needed to pay attention. Likewise, it changed your own body language as well.

The Cycle of Thoughts, Feelings, and Behaviors

This happens because human behavior exists within a cycle. Your thoughts influence your feelings, which influence your behaviors. This is quite simple to understand and is something that is highly recognized throughout psychology in general. Your thoughts are directly related to how you interpret the world around you. Largely, they are based on those subconscious judgments that you make as you navigate through the world. The more that you experience something without challenging it, the more that your subconscious mind comes to accept it. Your subconscious recognizes that your lack of correction is an effective agreement and, therefore, will react accordingly.

Your thoughts are powerful. They create the emotions that you feel. Have you ever been sitting somewhere and realized that you were frustrated or angry about something? You might not know why you are so angry at the moment, but you know that you are, and as a result, you have to stop and think closer about it. What is it that is pushing you to feel that way? You think about it and realize that ultimately, it is often due to something entirely unrelated to everything else that you are doing. This is imperative to remember—often, it is an entirely unrelated thought that was the problem all along that created so many issues for you. If you keep this in mind, you can start to see what it is that happens inside the mind of someone else.

Your emotions have a very important role—they serve to keep you motivated to respond to the situation that you are in. Each emotion will have its own evolutionary purpose that is related to keeping you alive. They all work together to provide those instinctive actions that you follow when you allow your emotions to rule you. This is important to keep in mind—it means that if you feel yourself feeling emotional and then motivated toward a specific action, it is probably for a reason. The emotions that you feel can be broken down into just seven:

- **Happiness:** You feel happy to motivate yourself to repeat that behavior again. It is something that was rewarding for some reason, and you instinctively want to reinforce it.
- **Sadness:** You feel sadness when you have done something that caused a loss of some sort. Usually, this is something such as someone got hurt or was lost. You feel sadness to remind yourself

that repeating that action would be problematic for several different reasons. It motivates you to seek comfort and help from others.
- **Anger:** Anger motivates you to fight back. Usually, it is the result of feeling threatened for some reason or another and is designed to cause you to protect yourself or those around you.
- **Fear:** Fear is your motivation to protect yourself from a threat that you cannot fight off. When you feel fear, you feel a need to escape at all costs. Fear may become angry if you have a way to conceivably fight your way out of the problem. It will usually lead to you attempting to find an out from a situation, or lashing out.
- **Surprise:** Surprise is your body's reaction to needing to pay more attention to whatever it is that is happening around you. It drives you to focus on whatever is in front of you so you can address the situation.
- **Contempt:** Contempt is the feeling that is meant to motivate you to avoid someone. It is effectively disgust and anger combined and directed to one person.
- **Disgust**: Disgust is meant to make you avoid something that is no good for you. You feel disgusted when you are exposed to something that is rotten, either literally or figuratively. It is meant to keep you away from the situation and far from getting involved with it. When you feel disgusted, you tell yourself that you must avoid whatever it is.

As you can see, your emotions have a very important purpose, and you owe it to yourself to understand them. These emotions become highly motivating and create behaviors if you are not attempting to consciously outweigh them. Yes, you can make it a point to change up your behaviors yourself, but it is not always that easy. If you don't know what you are doing, you can end up stuck. You can find yourself controlled by your emotions. However, this means that you can also typically look at what other people are doing to understand them as well. If you wanted to understand what is going on in someone else's mind, you would look at their behaviors because the behaviors will follow.

Think of it this way—if you see someone running toward you with a scowl and overall very threatening body language, you can assume that they are furious about something. Through understanding that they are furious, you can then look around and figure out what the problem is. Did you just cut him off in the parking lot? He might be annoyed that you snatched up a spot. Did you offend him somehow? If so, figure it out.

By being able to follow these patterns in this manner, you can help yourself to figure out what to do next. You can look at people and understand the mindsets that they are taking through everything that they do.

CHAPTER 3
The Uses Of Analyzing Others

When it comes to being able to analyze others, you have several key benefits that can help you, and there are several situations that you can use your analysis of others to help yourself as well. When you learn what it will take to analyze other people, you can then begin to utilize it as much as possible. The more that you utilize it, the more likely that you are to find a way that you can better the situation entirely. Think about it this way—you can stop and consider the fact that you are looking at the actions to read the minds of those around you. This is something that we have already made quite clear. Now, all you will need to do is make sure that you are taking the time to recognize the ways that this can benefit you.

In this chapter, we will address several key ways that you can utilize the ability to analyze others to help yourself in real-life scenarios. We will see several key uses that can benefit just about anyone. Whether you are introverted, extroverted, interested in other people, or not, being able to read people is a skill that everyone should have.

Better Negotiating

When you start to negotiate with people, you are setting out to come up with some sort of agreement between parties. You and someone else will be sitting down and walking through all of the steps of figuring out what it is that you want and where that common ground between you lies. It could be that you want one thing, and they want another, and you need to figure out which concessions that you are willing to make. However, it is difficult for you to ensure that your negotiations are on the right foot when you and the other person are not really willing to work with each other. This prevents you from being able to work well with everyone involved. However, what you can do is learn how you can better engage through being able to read body language.

Imagine this: You are sitting in front of the other person, and they do not appear to be very open to being negotiated with in the first place. Do you think that you are going to get very far? Perhaps they are sitting there, arms crossed, and looking away from you because they do not really want to engage. The chances are, they do not want to be involved with you at all- they do not want to have to deal with you, so they try to avoid doing so. They shut down their body language.

When you can see this in someone else, you can tell that they are not currently open to that negotiation in the first place. This means that what you can do is take the time that you will need to stop and think. You will be able to tell yourself that you do not want to deal with the situation, and you will not be as effective as if they were more open. You know this— and yet you are stuck. In this instance, the best thing that you can do is ensure that you are going to find a way to better engage. When you can find that best set of engagement, you can then begin to figure out what it will take to better encourage the other person to open up.

Through being able to read the other person, you can then begin to figure out how best to engage. You will figure out what it will take for you to actually talk to them. You will learn how you can actually properly interact with them. This is imperative—you will be able to ensure that ultimately, you are happier with the situation at hand. This matters immensely—you must make sure that you are in a position in which you can better engage. When you get to that point, you know that you will be able to negotiate more effectively. You have to learn how to open up their body language by using your own to influence them. Over time, you then get them to be more willing to engage with you, and as a result, you get to negotiate.

Better Selling

Similarly, you can use your ability to read people's body language to land sales. This is especially true if you find yourself working with someone that may not actually be as well informed about their own body language. If you find that you are looking at someone that appears to not be very familiar with their own body language, you can realize that you can actually tell more about their mindset than they can. This can be useful, for example, if you are attempting to convince them to buy something. By being able to tell what they think when they struggle with it themselves, you are able to start pinpointing what it is that they want.

Being able to read their body language also lets you know if you are on the right track to getting what they want right. Think about it—if you are selling a car, you would want to make sure that you are getting the right taste down for what they want. This means that you would want to make sure that you are paying attention to the reactions that they have as you are going through everything. You can tell by watching their body language closely whether they are actually interested in what you are showing them or if you are actually on the wrong track, and they are just trying to be polite. By being able to figure this out little by little, you can help yourself to figure out precisely what it is that you should be offering them.

Consider, for example, showing them a red minivan. You can tell by their reaction if they are enthusiastic about it, whether they need convincing, or if you are entirely on the wrong track. Being able to watch their reaction tells you whether you should redirect them to something else or if what is going to be best in this situation is going toward something else entirely. The more that you do this and the more you get used to reading the other person, the more likely that you are to actually successfully convince them of whatever it is that you are trying to convince them to buy.

This can be used in any sort of sales-based job. When you can tell what it is that will drive someone to purchase; you can take advantage of the situation. You will be able to get those sales just because you will know what it is that someone wants. Take, for example, the idea that people tend to orient themselves, so their feet point at what it is that they want at the moment. Most people do not realize this, and it is so unconscious anyway that they do not quite catch on to what they are doing. However, once you know this, you can look at the direction of the feet when you are regarding a customer. If you can see that their feet are pointing toward the exit, you can assume they want to go, whereas if you see their feet pointing in the direction of a certain item, you can presume that they want to approach it.

Better Interviewing Skills

When it comes to looking at interviewing skills, being able to read people is, once again, something that can be incredibly useful, whether you are the interviewer or the interviewee. When you are the one doing the interviewing, being able to read what the other person is thinking or feeling becomes highly important—it helps you to ensure that you are on the right track with the other person. It ensures that you are able to read just how confident or honest the other person is being. When it comes to seeing that confidence or honesty, you can tell a lot about someone. Imagine that you have just asked them to answer a question about a time that they were able to overcome a problem—if you know what you are looking for, you can identify when they are lying about if they are. You will also be able to tell if they are telling the truth. This means that you can be an incredibly intuitive interviewer that will help you to show yourself whether or not you are actually paying close attention to the situation. When you are able to tell what is going on with those that you interview, you can truly choose the strongest of the candidates because you can better and more comfortably read them.

Additionally, as someone that is on the other side of the situation, if you are the one being interviewed, you can tell just how well the interview is going by virtue of understanding the body language that goes into the situation as well. Being able to tell what they are thinking and feeling at any point in time is highly powerful. It will help you immensely to ensure that you can better cope with the situation that you are involved in. You can tell if you are losing interest form the interviewer or if the interviewer does not seem to like you much. The more that you are able to tell just how liked or disliked you are, the more likely you are to be able to get through the interview well. Think about it—you can use that reading of the other person's body language to help yourself to figure out precisely what it is that you will need to better the situation that you are in. When you learn how to identify what you are doing and how you are doing it, you realize that ultimately, you can tweak your body language to make yourself that much more attractive of an interviewer.

Being able to read each other in these situations where you are closely intertwined with each other becomes imperative—being able to show yourself that you do know what to expect and how to read the other people will set you up for success. This is crucial—if you want to thrive, then you want to ensure that you are putting yourself in a situation where you can do so.

Better Leadership Skills

people, you must make sure that you are paying close attention to the situation at hand. Finally, consider the boost to leadership skills when you know how to read people as well. If you have ever read a book on emotional intelligence, you would know that one of the most defining features of a good leader is someone that is able to understand and motivate the people that they are trying to lead. When you can read what someone else is thinking or feeling, you can ensure that everyone is on the same page, while also being able to defuse conflicts before they have a chance to get bad enough to cause problems. The more that you work with yourself, the more that you can realize that ultimately, you will be in a position where you can better engage. Think about it: If you are going to be trying to lead people, you need to ensure that you are in a position where you feel like you can tell what it is that the people around you are thinking or feeling. When it turns out that what they are feeling or thinking is positive, they will usually be more inclined to help or follow through with what you need.

Good leaders are those who are able to ensure that they are pushing people in the right direction for the right reason. When you are able to figure out what it is that drives them, you are able to see that they want to follow you. You will be able to make them feel confident in you, and that is how you know that you are effective. Ultimately, the best leaders will be able to read their followers and will take great pleasure in figuring out what they can do and how they can engage with everyone else.

Learning to read people can help when you are giving a speech to people; for example—you will be able to tell if people understand what you are saying or if you need to start changing up the level of difficulty that you will speak. It will help you to tell if people agree with what you are saying or if you are causing problems with the way that you are approaching a situation. Being able to tell what everyone else wants and thinks means that you will be able to better motivate people for this reason.

One on one, you can show that you are a good listener when you are analyzing body language—you will pick up on those nonverbal cues as well that will help you to figure out what it will take for you to better get along with those around you. When you can better relate to everyone involved, you will show yourself that you can better speak to them. You will be able to show yourself that you are someone that is more capable of navigating through these situations. You will show yourself precisely what you must do if you want to be able to engage well with those around you.

Ultimately, being able to read other people becomes something that is highly beneficial to you. If you want to be able to understand what is going on in the minds of others, you must learn to read their body language so you can begin to understand them as individuals as well as better. The more that you can do this, the better that you will do in engaging with those around you.

Analyzing other people, then, becomes one of your most crucial tools when it comes to being able to better yourself and your interactions with people. If you want to do well, you must make sure that you are taking the time to better the situation to the best of your ability. The more that you do this, the better the situation will be.

CHAPTER 4
Looking At Nonverbal Cues

Understanding what other people are thinking or feeling starts with looking at the nonverbal. It starts by looking at how people behave and what their bodies are saying without listening to the words. Nonverbal communication might be more primitive than directly stating what you are thinking or feeling, but that doesn't make it any less effective—after all, nature has used nonverbal cues for millennia in animals. The entirety of social animals communicate nonverbally—they have all sorts of different ways that they are able to get their points across. Even bees have a complex form of communication through their movements that allow other bees to know where they need to go.

Nonverbal communication makes up the bulk of any communication that you will do, and that is what makes it so important to use and understand. It is something that you must learn to understand so you *can* see what is going on behind the scenes. For this reason, we will dedicate this chapter to going over what nonverbal communication is, what to look at when trying to understand it, and how to read it. When it comes to being able to read other people, you are looking for how they move.

Defining Nonverbal Communication

Defining nonverbal communication is simple: It is communication that your body does nonverbally. This means that it happens without words. However, there is more to it than just that—nonverbal communication is unconscious. When you communicate nonverbally, your body will create cues that are sent to those around you. People around you then are able to receive those signals that you send out and translate and understand them.

Your communication with other people does consist of the words that you say, but there is more to it as well. The minuscule movements that you make are interpreted by the people around you without them being aware of it. That's what causes people to get those gut feelings about others when they were talking. If you've ever had that feeling when talking to someone that they were lying, you've had it before. You know that feeling—that sensation that you are in a position in which someone is going to be dangerous, or when someone is problematic in other ways. Likewise, you can see when they're more amicable as well. Being able to understand that nonverbal communication is critical, and your mind reads it without thinking about it. You can tell when someone is threatening no matter where they are from. You can tell when someone is happy to see you, regardless of their culture or place of origin. This is because we can all read very similar body language. We know that certain movements are aggressive, even innately. Your body knows this, as makes your mind and your unconscious mind makes it a point to go through everything.

Of course, it is important to note that nonverbal language can also take the place of sounds that are made. Groaning or sighing, for example, involves making sounds, but there are no words that are formed. It is nonverbal for that reason alone. Verbal communication involves the utilization of words in several forms, from being able to write something down to speaking it out loud. Nonverbal communication, then, is anything else. If it is not filled up with words, it is nonverbal communication. When you start to recognize nonverbal communication as actually making up the bulk of everything that we convey to each other, you start recognizing just how powerful it is.

What to Look at for Nonverbal Language

When it comes to being able to read nonverbal communication, there are a few easy places that you can look—when you are reading it in other people, there are a handful of things to consider. Each of the different kinds of nonverbal communication becomes imperative for you to be able to discuss. These different forms of nonverbal communication that you ought to pay attention to are kinesics, oculesics, haptics, proxemics, and vocalics.

Kinesics

Kinesics refers to the general body language that you display at any point in time. It is the movements, the general expressions, and the demeanor that your body takes on. This is kinesthetic—referring to movement. When you keep this in mind, you can keep track of what it is with ease. The bulk of what you will be learning to read in this book is kinesic in nature just due to the fact that there are so many more kinesic factors that come into play when it comes to looking at nonverbal body language.

Oculesics

Oculesics refers to the movements of the eyes. While it is technically indicative of a form of kinesics, it is also quite focused, and for that reason, it gets its own special consideration. It is the ability to understand the movements of eyes in general, from how they open, close, gaze at things, and more. This is imperative to understand so you can be certain that you can read the windows to the soul, as they are commonly referred to.

Haptics

Haptics allows you to utilize touch to communicate. Different touches can convey widely different concepts, especially when you consider the ways that touch can vary so dramatically. Touch can go from something that you use to gently encourage someone to push them away or lashing out at them. Even a brief touch can be enough to communicate something important, and that must be considered heavily.

Proxemics
Proxemics refers to the utilization of space in order to communicate topics or concepts. It can be both vertical and horizontal, referring to how you position yourself above or around someone else. When you look at proxemics, you are looking at how a boss may attempt to tower over a person that is being scolded, or how someone who is uninterested in someone else will stand further away from them.

Vocalics
Finally, vocalics refers to the way in which you use your voice to communicate nonverbally. It consists of how you talk to others, what you do with them around, or how you make sounds. Laughing, groaning, sighing, screeching, humming, and other such sounds are all examples of nonverbal communication that you can use with others, and they all involve you being able to communicate something.

All of these come together to create the nonverbal communication that you use—they are important to consider. They all matter to ensure that you can better understand and even influence other people, and we will be working on learning to read this. Nonverbal communication is an integral part of being able to communicate in general, and without it, you cannot hope to understand the full picture that you hear when you are interacting. You will not see everything for what things are when you cannot communicate or see what the undertones are. You must be able to read those undertones so you can be certain that you do understand what is going on.

Learning to Read People
Reading other people is something that you will need to learn to be successful in many different situations, and thankfully, it doesn't have to be hard. With just a few steps, you can begin to understand what is going on in other people's minds so you can then begin to interpret their actions and feelings. Your own actions and feelings will be influenced by other people—and because of that, being able to read theirs as well becomes imperative. Thankfully, you can follow this guide:

Step 1: Identify personality type
To begin understanding the people around you, you must start with determining the personality type of the other person. There are all sorts of ways that you can do this, but the easiest is to identify a few simple factors that come into play as you watch someone. You will be watching how they navigate as well as how they respond. In looking at this, you will start to understand the kind of person that you are exposed to.

First, consider the difference between sensing or being intuitive. This is the first difference that you will be looking at. Some people tend to orient themselves with the use of their senses—they look for support and facts that help others end up being more intuitive in nature- they focus on what it is that they are feeling at any point in time. This is imperative to pay attention to. When you watch the personality type and pay attention to how someone chooses to navigate in the world, you start to see new patterns. You see into their minds and how they think—this is imperative to recognize their behaviors. This beginning point will provide that insight for you.

Then, you must consider whether they react to the world through thoughts or feelings. Are they focusing on making sure that they satisfy their emotions? Are they looking for ways for them to feel content? Are they looking for ways to think about their situations? Thinking individuals tend to be more driven by their own rationality and logic than anything else—they will intentionally respond to the world through following preset and predetermined rules. They are more likely to abide by those rules. Feeling individuals, on the other hand, are driven by their emotions. They consider values and the situation at hand rather than trying to force it into a situation that I can naturally fall into.

When you start to consider this, you can then address whether the person that you are speaking to is introverted or extroverted. The introverts are those that seem to orient themselves within themselves—they are quieter because they are caught up in their own thoughts and feelings at the time. They focus on themselves and how they behave, and they often find themselves drained being around other people too much. They are more likely to be quietly observing when they are in a group, and they look like they may be overwhelmed when they are pushed into the limelight.

Extroverts, on the other hand, tend to love being the center of attention. They love to be around other people to interact—they feel the best when they are able to engage well with others. They act rather than think, and they are usually much more at ease in social settings.

Step 2: Get the base reading of their body language

Then, when you have that base reading of what kind of person you are trying to read, you can start focusing on getting a base reading. It is important to know what is going on in their mind before getting started so you can tell whether what is happening appears to be characteristic or not. Think about it—an introvert probably would not be running around with their hands up in the air for no reason, and an extrovert probably would not be averting their gaze in a conversation. Understanding this will help you to begin to read the base body language to figure out just how natural it is.

Getting the base reading of someone else's body language becomes incredibly important before you start reading. This will give you a general guideline to understanding what is going on inside the mind of the other person. Think about it—if you are driving your car and realize that you are getting 20 miles to the gallon, how would you feel about it? Would you think that is a good thing or a bad thing? The answer is entirely dependent upon the base MPG that you expect. A truck getting 20 miles to the gallon may actually be somewhat decent—many of them are notorious gas guzzlers. A brand new Prius only getting 20 miles to the gallon, on the other hand, is indicative that something is catastrophically wrong—the MPG is almost halved. This consideration is important: You must be able to understand what is going on, but you also have to have that context as well. You must be able to tell whether what is happening is actually a good or a bad thing by comparing it to the natural state.

In terms of body language, that means taking a look at natural states. If you want to read someone well as you engage, you must see their default body language before you begin. This is most often done either by watching the other person interact without any pressure or by having a general basic conversation with someone else if you are getting ready to try to read them. During that general basic conversation, make it a point to pay close attention to how they engage with you. How are they holding themselves? What are they doing with themselves? Pay attention to their demeanor and figure out how they are more likely to stand.

Step 3: Look for discrepancies in their body language

Next, consider looking for any discrepancies. This happens during the interaction now- when you go through the motions and start looking at how you engage with each other, you start to see where those discrepancies begin and what they mean. Looking at those means that you will be able to see the different behaviors. This is where their body language will begin to tell you everything that you need to know. You will be able to see how the person is engaging with you during your interaction. Are they uncharacteristically being shy? Are they averting their eyes a lot? Are they batting their eyes at you? Start looking for the signs. Start looking around at how they behave. Note anything that does not match up with the original baseline body language that you identified and make sure that you take the time and effort to pay closer attention to it.

Step 4: Identify the clusters of behaviors

Next, you must start building up clusters of behaviors. This is where you start to consider the context of the body language that you see. Are they averting their eyes because they are scared or because they are lying to you? You may need to look at other body languages to see exactly what is going on with them. By beginning to understand those different clusters of behavior, you can then begin to understand what you are doing and how you are doing it. You will be able to understand how everything plays out together.

For example, imagine a woman who is looking down at the floor. She could be nervous, shy, or also just uncomfortable. She could be embarrassed as well. What you need to pay attention to, then, is everything else alongside it. You need to look for the other signs to tell the difference. Someone who is nervous may also cross their arms and shift in hopes of being able to self-soothe, or someone who is embarrassed may also be blushing uncontrollably and stuttering. You need to look at other signs to see what is going on.

When it comes to identifying clusters of behaviors, you will want to pay attention to whether you see the same behaviors play out over and over again. You are looking for signs that the behaviors are repeating over and over again, that they are not just one-off coincidences. Being sure that you are considerate of this point will help you to ensure that you can get the cleanest reading possible.

Step 5: Interpreting the clusters of behaviors

Finally, the last step in all of this is making sure that you analyze it. Look at the behaviors, the feelings, and then start to figure out why they are what they are. Pay attention to the way that people tend to engage. Consider the situation that they are in. Does their reaction make sense? Do they seem like they are out of proportion? All of these factors will help you to figure out what you should be doing and how you should be taking the behaviors that you are exposed to. The sooner that you learn how to read those behaviors, the sooner you can start to interpret them.

CHAPTER 5
Understanding The Movements Of The Face

For the most part, when people think about reading others, they look to the face. They think that if they are going to be reading anything about the other person, it will happen by looking at the expressions that they make. This is true to some degree—the face will almost always be the first place people look just instinctively. If you are talking to someone, you naturally look at their face when you are trying to figure out their thoughts that they have. When you do this, you are checking out several different aspects—you are looking at them in the eye, which acknowledges they are there. However, you will also be looking at them in several other ways as well. You will see their eyebrows and mouth as well while looking at their general expression in hopes of getting more information about them.

Ultimately, the face is one of the easiest places to start—but it is also the one place that people will tend to control when they want to hide their emotions. If you see that someone is trying to lie, they will almost always betray themselves in the face—they will know to try to alter their facial expressions in an attempt to lie to you. While this is a great starting point, you will need to remember that it must be taken in tandem with all other aspects of facial features and expressions, as we will explain throughout the book.

Within this chapter, we have a few key objectives: We will be identifying the universal expressions that you can expect to see no matter the person. We will then go body part by body part on the face to start looking at common body language. In particular, we will be discussing the eyes, the eyebrows, the forehead, the cheeks, the lips, and the mouth.

Universal Expressions

Did you know that there are several expressions that humans make that are universal? There are seven of them that are common across all cultures. They are commonly referred to as universal expressions, and they help to support the idea that there are certain emotions that are largely universal as well regardless of culture. These universal expressions are precisely what they may sound like—they will be identified by anyone around the world no matter where they come from, and they can actually be found in blind individuals that have never actually seen another person's face before.

If this sounds impossible, think about dogs. If you take a newborn puppy from its mother and raise it, there are certain aspects of its body language that are universal—they will happen whether they know the meaning of the wag or not. We, like dogs, have our own set of universal body language. After all, if you take a dog from the US and drop it off in Japan, it will still be able to communicate with the other dogs through body language. Likewise, your expressions will be recognized no matter where in the world that you go.

Happiness

The emotion of happiness is felt when you have met your needs or done something that is satisfying or pleasant. Generally speaking, happiness is expressed through relaxed and sometimes even excited body language. There may be a smile that bares teeth, or the mouth may be closed with lips turned upward. Either way, however, you are looking out for the Duchenne smile—the real smile where the corners of the eyes begin to crinkle. This is how you know that happiness is legitimate and not meant to just throw you off. Additionally, you may see that the eyebrows are pulled up as well.

Sadness

Sadness is perhaps the hardest of the emotions to fake—it is something that has very distinctive features. In particular, you can expect to see that the eyebrows will lower with the inner corners raising upward and pulling together. This causes a wrinkling effect between and above the brows. Additionally, you will see that the jaw pulls upwards while the bottom lip pouts outward at the same time.

Anger

Anger is going to involve the entire face. When you face an angry person, you will see them lower their eyebrows together while also pulling them inward to furrow into a V shape. The eyelids will usually tense up around the eyes, which stare harshly. Additionally, you can expect to see the lips being forced together into a thin line, or they may be open with the mouth in a square shape. The jaw, when closed, maybe either tense or jutting out.

Fear

Fear is identifiable by the eyebrows as they pull up and together at the center of the forehead. This creates a worrying furrow, and the brows themselves flatten instead of arching out. As this happens, you will note that the eyelid above the eyes is what rises upward to allow for access to seeing the whites above the iris rather than below. At the same time, the mouth is typically open with lips that pull back.

Surprise

Surprise can sometimes be mistaken for fear, largely because of the fact that you can see the whites of the eyes with both. However, with surprise, you should expect to see the whites all around the iris instead of just above. Additionally, you will expect to see some wrinkling along the forehead with an open, slack jaw lacking tension. The brows will arch and curve as they raise up, and usually, the skin between the brow and the eye is stretched taut.

Contempt
When you see contempt in someone else, you usually notice it because they raise up just one side of the mouth and eyebrow. It is a quick flash of a sneer, usually only lasting a second or two before it disappears.

Disgust
Disgust has a very important design for the expression that can help you to remember it. In disgust, you can expect to see the face all coming inward to protect your eyes, nose, and mouth, all of which are quite sensitive and require protection to ensure that they do not get damaged from toxins of any kind. The eyebrows lower to shield your eyes while your lips pull upward while your nose wrinkles in an attempt to protect the nose. The cheeks will also squeeze upward to help shield the eyes.

Reading the Eyes
Eyes are commonly called the windows to your soul for a reason—they are incredibly expressive. When you glance at someone else's eyes, you do a few important things. One, you acknowledge that they are there and present. This is majorly important—when you do this, you show them that you are actively paying attention to them. You show that you are actively watching to show that you are giving them your attention. Being able to pay attention to the eyes usually comes with its own benefits by taking the time to read the gaze, pupil dilation, and the amount of eye contact that is made.

Reading Gaze
The gaze will tell you an awful lot about the person that you are looking at. In particular, there are two key aspects that you will want to consider when attempting to read the gaze of someone else. You must look at the location and the duration. However, when you learn to understand how to read this part of the body, you can get a clear idea of what is going on in someone else's mind.

- **Location of the gaze:** if you see that someone is looking at something, there is a good chance that they want it. A glance at the door says that someone is done talking while staring down a piece of cake can imply that the cake is the object of desire at that moment. When you learn to follow someone else's gaze, you can usually figure out what it is that has drawn attraction and then figure out whether the attention is good or bad by looking at the rest of the body language
- **Duration of the gaze:** The amount of time spent staring at something is also indicative of important points as well. When you look at the duration of someone else's gaze toward something else, you start to figure out what it will take to understand what they are doing and thinking. You want to ensure that you know that they are directly driven by whatever it is that they are looking at. Typically, the longer that someone stares at something, the

more important it is to them or the more interesting that they find it.

Reading eye contact

When you want to read eye contact with someone else, you want to keep in mind that generally speaking, eye contact is something that can be quite intense. It can be very rapidly construed as wrong or too forceful and direct if you do not know what you are doing. However, not enough eye contact is also deemed problematic as it implies that you are not actually interested or that you are lying about something. Just the right amount of eye contact is having eye contact, roughly 70% of the time. Keep in mind that if you stare too much, you will be deemed aggressive, and that will give you the exact opposite of what you are trying to achieve.

Reading pupil dilation

Pupil dilation occurs when the pupils of the eyes start to expand. However, it is also quite difficult to notice if you are not right next to someone else or if you find that they have an eye color that is darker and will help to obscure the pupil. However, if you look at the eyes closed, you may be able to identify when the pupils are dilated. The thing about pupil dilation is that it is impossible to falsify—there is no way for you to consciously control the dilation of your pupils, and as such, it is something that is fairly reliable to use.

Typically, pupils will dilate when you look at someone or something that you want or are attracted to. When you find something more attractive, you will usually have more dilation of the pupil. It is also the case, however, that the pupils will dilate in response to mental processing as well. If you are trying to do complex math, for example, the pupils will dilate as a result.

Reading the Eyebrows

The eyebrows have a lot to say about the people that they belong to. They sort of frame the eyes and create an additional degree of expression. When you take a look at the eyebrows, you see that arch over the eyes that are free to move in most directions. In particular, you will find that looking at the eyebrows will tell you a lot. Take a look at the following signs.

Raised

Raising the brows tends to imply that you want to absorb more of your surroundings. You may be raising them to see more or to also emphasize something that you want to ask as well. It could, for example, create a need to convey a question or to show doubt over a situation as well.

Raising inner corners

By raising the inner corners of your eyebrows, especially when you pull them together in the center, you show either anxiety or relief. You will have to look at other signs to determine which is more appropriate in this instance.

Lowered

When you lower your eyebrows, you are hooding your eyes, as if you are hiding them from view. You are also showing that your line of sight has honed in on one thing, in particular, implying that you are highly focused on whatever it is that you are staring at. This is typically indicative of annoyance or dominance, though it can also show anger depending upon the other signs of the face as well.

Lowering center

When it comes to taking a look at the center of the brows, they can sometimes furrow together to make a V shape. When this happens, there are slight wrinkles there that create the shape in the first place. Usually, this is a sign of concentration or potential frustration.

Lowering and raising repeatedly

When the brows come up and down repeatedly, especially rapidly, you are wiggling them. This typically either wants to get attention from someone else or even acknowledge that they are present. You can also use it to show an exaggerated shock.

Reading the Cheeks

Cheeks make up the bulk of your face, and yet they are often forgotten when it comes time to read body language. However, they are quite important to pay attention to, and you will want to focus on them to the best of your ability. Ultimately, looking at the cheeks will help you to figure out what you are doing when also considering other body parts at the same time. When you learn to read the cheeks, you will get an extra glimpse into the mindset of the other person.

Cheeks pulled in

When cheeks are pulled in, you can usually assume that the other person is feeling annoyed, especially if you can also see signs of the lips being pursed as well. This is highly important to consider, as well. You usually want to avoid bothering someone if they are like this.

Cheeks blown out

If you see that their cheeks are blown outward, you see them expanding them out. They are puffed, and this typically happens out of sheer exaggeration as a sign of being unsure what to do next or feeling like you are somewhat overwhelmed with everything that you have to get done. When you consider this action, you usually are showing signs of great disapproval.

Cheeks turning red

When cheeks begin to turn red, it is usually out of embarrassment or anger over a situation. Look for other cues that can help you to clarify what they seem to be thinking.

Cheeks paling
When cheeks start to turn pale on the other hand, you can see that the blood has rushed out of their faces. This usually shows that the blood has redirected elsewhere, such as into the legs to run. It is often a sign of fear or uncertainty. However, it could also be a sign that it is simply cold outside.

Chewing on the inside of the cheek
When you chew on the inside of your cheek, you imply that you are nervous about the current situation for some reason. You show that you are a bit uncertain about how everything is going, and it is a form of trying to self-soothe. It can also be a sign of trying to avoid speaking words that you know will cause problems, such as words that would deceive your lies that you are telling.

Touching the cheek
By touching your cheek, you are showing signs of exaggeration or emphasis over something that is happening. Usually, both hands on both cheeks show exaggeration and surprise over something, or it could also be horror.

Reading the Forehead
The forehead will tell you vast amounts about what you can expect to understand about another person. While the forehead cannot really move much, it still can do many different things, such as wrinkles or sweat and this can be quite telling on its own. Most people tend to ignore it, but professional gamblers, who know that everything hinges upon them being able to bluff their way to their victories that they are looking for, will make it a point to hide their foreheads as much as possible to prevent others from knowing what they are thinking.

Wrinkled
When a forehead is wrinkled, this is usually due to a movement of the eyebrows. Typically, when you see someone with a wrinkled forehead, you can assume that they are emphasizing whatever they are making the eyebrows do or say. If you see that someone is furrowing their brows and their forehead wrinkles as well, it is like extreme disapproval or an extreme focus.

Sweaty
When you notice that the forehead is sweaty on someone else, there can be a few different reasons for it. They may find that they are exercising too much, and as a result, they are sweating. The temperatures in the area may also genuinely be too hot as well. However, more likely than not, if the temperatures are not to blame, then it can apply either fear or arousal.

Touching the forehead

By touching one's forehead, you can read that they are trying to remove sweat. This is usually a signal that they are relieved about something, whether that something is a job finally completed or relief of a problem that they were going to have to face. When you touch your forehead, it could also be a sign of fear in which you are struggling to overcome. On the other hand, it could also be saluting someone to show respect or touching the head to imply thought.

Reading the Mouth and the Lips

When it comes to reading the mouth and lips, you can get a whole wealth of information relatively simply. All you have to do is pay attention to the way that the mouth and lips move, and you are able to start making out a lot of different types of emotions.

Flattening lips

When lips flatten together, you show that you are trying to hold your tongue—you want to avoid saying something. It could be that you disapprove but also would rather not offend the other person, or you may also feel like you need to speak but know that it is not the right place or time. Either way, it can be highly problematic if you see this. Assume that the other person does not have something nice to say.

Lowering lips down

When lips are pulled down, you usually are seeing some degree of sadness or displeasure that must be acknowledged. This is typically seen in a frown or a grimace of some sort and is indicative of that dislike of whatever else is going on.

Parting lips

Parting lips is highly important as well. When you see this, you know that the other person is flirting with you. This is even more the case when you can see that they are making gentle, coy eye contact with you or if you see their tongue coming out as well. However, this can also be indicative of simply wanting to talk to someone else while waiting for their attention.

Puckering lips

When you pucker lips, you show that you are not very certain about something that is happening. You have some reason to disagree with or dislike it.

Pursing lips

Pursing your lips is slightly different from puckering. While puckering is a kissing motion, pursing your lips involves pulling them in and closed. It is usually indicative of some degree of tension, and you will need to turn to the rest of the body language as well to figure it out.

Raising lips up
When you see lips pulled up, there is usually a reason for it—and for the most part, it is positive. It is usually a smile, though it could also indicate feelings of disgust if you see other telltale signs of it.

Sucking on lips
When you suck your lips in, you pull them into your mouth to hide the pinkness of them. This is typically a sign of thinking and uncertainty though it can certainly also be a sign that you are trying to suppress something.

CHAPTER 6
Understanding The Movements Of The Body

At this point, it is time to start looking at the body and how you move it in general. We all hold our posture differently, and that posture that we have is always going to be indicative of the feelings that we have at the moment. Our posture is constantly shifting with our moods. You may be standing tall one moment, only to have the entire demeanor shift as soon as something frightening happens. When you see that someone else's body language is shifting a lot, you can use that to interpret what is happening around you.

Within this chapter, we have several key concepts to go over—we must identify open vs. closed body language first so we can then get through the rest of the chapter. Then, we will look at how some people move their bodies in open and closed manners. In particular, this chapter is focused on reading the arms, hands, and shoulders to begin creating that foundation to go along with the expressions that we looked at in the previous chapter.

Open Vs. Closed Body Language

Understanding the difference between open and closed body language is imperative. This is the most fundamental way to understand the behavior that you are exposed to just due to the fact that the language that you view will be predominantly either open or closed. Open body language signals that you are open to some sort of interaction with the other person—it conveys a receptiveness to being approached. Typically, open body language is positive, but it can be negative as well. In fact, aggression is often very open body language because it involves approaching another person. It will have a wider stance that you commonly see with open body language because of this. It is an openness to violence.

Closed body language, then, tells you that they do not want to engage with someone at all. It shows an attempt to close oneself off from the interaction entirely or to find a way to escape it. When you have closed body language, you are trying to retreat rather than approach the situation that you have at hand. This difference is imperative to understand—when you are closed off to others, you are trying to avoid that interaction entirely.

Usually speaking, open body language is relaxed and wider. It is more natural and at ease—it shows a calmness or a recognition that there is going to be an argument or a fight. It shows that there will be no escalation from the individual in particular. Conversely, closed body language is closed off—it often involves barriers or creating barriers with your body, such as using hair to obscure the face, a hat rim to cover the eyes, or even just arms in front of the chest to avoid being forced to interact further. It is uncomfortable and desperate for closure.

When you want to address the differences between open and closed body language, you want to look for signs of that receptiveness in general. You will be looking to see if eye contact is being made if they are trying to close themselves off, or if they are even positioning themselves in such a way that they would not be involved with you. Being able to see the differences in this is imperative: It requires you to understand just how likely an interaction is to go well or poorly. It requires an acknowledgment, a recognition that the other person has their own preferences and opinions and that those ought to be considered as well.

Reading Shoulders

We will begin at the top of the arms—the shoulders. When we read the shoulders, we are taking a look at what they are doing in relation to the body—are they held inward, outward, or neutral? Are they moving? Are they resting against something else? Pay attention to the ways that the shoulders are sitting if you want to start understanding whether someone's body language is open or closed. Generally speaking. However, you can assume that someone is closed off if they are tucking their arms inward toward themselves. If their shoulders are held tightly, it is probably due to closing of the body language.

Exaggerated shrugging

When you shrug with exaggeration, you are raising and rotating your shoulders around in a circle. You are preparing for some sort of battle, and it shows that you are aggressive in some way, shape, or form. When you do this, you are showing signs that you are potentially becoming threatening.

Leaning on a shoulder

When you lean on one shoulder, you pose yourself against a wall. This is showing a sign of comfort and relaxation. You are making yourself vulnerable because it will take precious time to push yourself out of that position, and that means that you would leave yourself open to being hurt if that was the desire of the other person. It is also a common sign of dominance or confidence because it shows that you have little concern that something is going to go wrong or that you should be worried about being in a vulnerable position. You think that you will be just fine, so you shift into this position in which you are not ready to fight back if necessary.

Relaxed shoulders

Keeping your shoulders relaxed shows that you are comfortable or relaxed. It shows that there is little tension that is holding you back and that you are not concerned about the current situation that you find yourself in. You may show that your arms are low and unimpeded as they swing about by gravity. This is the ultimate indicator of relaxation.

Shrugging
Generally speaking, shrugging is a sign of ambivalence or being unsure about a situation. It may be that you do not know how to answer, or you could just not care about it. Especially when you move with your palms upright and exposed, you show that you are being honest and not hiding anything as you navigate the situation.

Subtle shrugging
Subtle shrugging involves you raising and dropping your shoulders rapidly, but slightly at the same time. It could even just be a quick shift of your arms and nothing else. It shows that you are uncertain about a situation or that you are uncaring about it. It could also be a sign of lying about something.

Turning shoulders away
When your shoulders are turned away from someone else, you position yourself so your body is facing away, even if you are still looking at the person. It implies that you are done with the conversation or interaction. You are waiting for it to wrap up so you can walk away and be done with it entirely.

Reading Arms
When it comes to reading the arms, there are even more movements that can occur than when considering the shoulders. This is thanks to increased levels of dexterity. Generally speaking, the more dexterous a body part, the more likely that it is to have even more types of movements.

Crossing arms
Crossing arms creates an immediate barrier between yourself and the person across from you. This is one of the clearest signs of showing that you are entirely uninterested in interacting with the people around you. When you look at how to understand these crossed arms, you see someone that wants to create some sort of distance or shield between themselves and the other person. Consider this person closed off and work on opening them up little by little.

Expanding arms outward
When arms are expanded outward, you are doing one of a few things. It could be that you are showing that you are comfortable with the current situation. You want to display that comfort to other people, and you want to portray that you are willing to be open. Or, it could be that you are showing dominance or even aggression, depending on the other actions that happen as well. All things considered, however, it is a genuine form of open body language that must be interpreted as such.

Hiding arms
When you hide your arms, you try to cover them up somehow. It could be that you pull them away, or you shift them so they can be rested behind

your back. It can show defensiveness if you pull away, or it could be confident if you are simply sitting there with your hands resting behind your back without a care in the world. Either way, you must look at the fact that you are showing that degree of confidence.

Pulling arms inward
When you pull your arms inward, you are shrinking away from an interaction. You are withdrawing yourself, trying to get away from it. This is textbook closed body language and shows a lack of willingness to proceed with the interaction. This should be taken quite seriously.

Raising arms above head
By raising your arms up in the air, you make yourself larger. You may be exaggerating your motion, or you could also be aggressive. Look at the rest of the body language that you are showing and then make it a point to put them together. You can usually assume that this is some sort of accentuation of whatever the rest of the body language is showing as well.

Reaching out
When you reach out toward someone else, the way to read it is entirely based on intent, along with the amount of force used. Generally speaking, intent to harm someone else is going to be very forceful reaching out, whereas if someone is much more gentle and careful as they reach out, they are usually making it a point to show comfort or kindness instead. Pay attention to the type of reaching out.

Self-hugging
Self-hugging is typically an attempt to self-soothe. Think about the look— you are reaching out and holding your side with one of your arms. You are showing that you are closed off and that you are attempting to calm down. You are trying to find a way to relax more so you can begin to engage more, or you are trying to hold it together long enough to get out of a situation that might not necessarily be as good as you want it to be.

Using arms as weapons
When you use your arms as weapons, you are making it clear that you are uninterested in being involved with those around you. You are making it clear that you are seeking space for yourself. You are lashing out at others. It could be in self-defense, or you could also be the instigator. This is entirely dependent upon the situation. However, it does show signs of aggression. The arms can be used as a club with a fist. It can slap. It can punch or jab. The hands are potent weapons that can be used strongly against other people.

Reading Hands
Finally, when you take a look at the hands-on people, you start to see so much more potential in their movements and actions. People generally try to hide their hands; however—hands are easy to read, and most

people know this. However, if you learn to pay close attention, you can spot all the signs that there could be a problem that you must address.

Chopping hands through air

When you chop your hands through the air, you have your hand flat, and you slice it through the air. Sometimes, you will make it a point to hit the edge of your hand against the palm of your other hand. It is meant to show dominance. This is especially the case if you do so with your palms down. However, if you chop your hand with palms up, it can imply that you are trying to get people to agree to your credibility.

Clasping hands together

When you clasp your hands together, you are holding your own hands. This is typically indicative of restraint or an attempt to calm yourself down. It is supposed to show that you are trying to be steady. Usually, it is regarded as closed off behavior, especially if the hands are tense as they sit there.

Hands hidden

When hands are hidden, it is indicative of you trying to hide something. You are attempting to put your hands out of sight so they cannot be read—perhaps behind your back or in your pockets. This is quite closed off and shows potential for deception, or it could also be intense submissiveness as well.

Hands tightened in fists

When you tighten your hands into a fist, you show firmness when they are at your sides. It could even be deemed aggressive if you show other aggressive behavior as well. You will need to make the context clear to determine whether it is just stubbornness or if it is going to bridge over to overt aggression.

Hands on hips

Putting your hands onto your hips is usually showing openness. Though it is commonly misinterpreted as aggression or being forceful, it is actually a position of readiness for whatever is about to happen. It shows that you are willing to do whatever you have to in the future.

Height of the thumb

When you take a look at the thumbs, you can see that confidence is usually noted by having higher thumbs. Think about how you can grip your arms when you cross them. If your thumb is extended and put outward, it shows that you are pointing them upwards aggressively.

Holding onto something

When you hold onto something, you usually create some sort of shield or barrier for yourself. Think of the look of putting a phone or a cup of coffee between yourself and someone else. You might hold onto it in front of yourself, trying to make it, so there is something between you and the other person.

Pointing
Pointing is typically considered to be rude, but it is also an indicator of dominance and of aggression in some situations. It shows a sign that you are more in control of a situation or that you are asserting that you are above someone else. Think of how you may scold a young child with the use of a finger to point. It is meant to show sternness and scolding.

Showing hands visibly with palms pointing down
When you put hands out, showing them openly, but do so with the palms down, you are showing that you are in control of the situation. You are making it clear that you control what is happening and that you refuse to make any changes to what you are doing. You show that you are firm in the situation, but you also show that you are trying to be forthcoming about everything as well. This is often seen when you look at politicians or leaders trying to talk to a crowd.

Showing hands visibly with palms pointing up
When you show hands visibly with the palms pointing upward, you are showing signs of honesty. In particular, it is a plea for trust, showing that there is nothing that you are attempting to hide in that particular situation that you are in. You are showing that you wish to be deemed as being honest in the moment. This is commonly seen with pastors or priests during a sermon.

Steepling fingers
When you steeple your fingers together, your fingers are pressed against each other at the pads, though the palms and finger lengths never touch. It is very similar to the look of a roof steeple above someone. It is meant to show confidence and authority. It is a clear sign of dominance when you see this. It will usually be seen by leaders around a table, almost calculatingly.

The temperature of the hands
The temperature that your hands take on actually tells a lot about what is being felt in the moment. When your hands are colder, usually, the entire body is tense. This is because when you are stressed out, your body redirects blood to important areas such as your heart and lungs, while also filling the legs so you can run. However, when the hands are warmer, it usually shows signs of relaxing. This becomes even more relevant when you start looking at haptics.

Widened hands
When the hands are wide, you show comfort. This means that if you can see individual gaps between each of the fingers, or the hands are simply spaced out widely. This is usually noted by seeing the large width between fingers as they stretch out. When hands are narrower, it shows stress.

CHAPTER 7
Understanding The Movements Of The Legs And Feet

Next comes looking at the feet and legs to begin to understand people. Despite the truth, most people disregard the feet and legs as not mattering much for body language. After all, all they do is hold you in one place. They just keep you there, not doing anything at all. They don't move about. They simply stand there, supporting you.

But, the truth is that they are actually highly telling. Though there are not too many different positions that legs can go into—your ankle and knees only bend one direction. However, you can pose them in several different ways, from sitting crisscross to standing up or leaning from one foot to the next. You can do all of that with ease. These different poses can actually portray an awful lot about who you are, what you are doing, and why you are doing what you do.

However, reading the legs and feet requires a bit more nuance. It requires you to pay attention to more than just how the legs are posed. Men and women actually differ quite a bit in how they stand themselves around and what they do with their legs. This means that you must be willing to pay attention to this—you will need to make sure that you are looking at how someone is posing and then also considering their gender as well to get the clearest details as to what is going on with them.

Within this chapter, we are going to go over many different ways that people stand and sit. When it is specific to just one gender, it will be noted. When it is nonspecific, that, too, will be noted. We will look at both open and closed off body language from the waist down, both in sitting poses and in standing as well. This is the best way to ensure that you get a clear understanding of the body language with it all separated out nice and easily.

Reading Standing Legs in Open Positions
When it comes to reading legs in a standing position, you must take a look at what they are doing. Standing legs really do not have many options just by virtue of the fact that they do have to support your body. They can really only do that in so many different ways when you are standing up. However, there are still a few different ways that you can look at the movement of the body that will help you to figure out what to do or how to read the movements that you make or how other people move.

Neutral stance
The neutral stance is one in which people stand with their feet spaced evenly apart, usually right around shoulder-width. This is the pose that is used to convey relaxation and comfort. When it comes to looking at this pose, you can assume that the other person is perfectly content and comfortable with the situation.

Weight on one foot
When weight is just on one foot, it shows more relaxation. It is indicative that the individual that you are speaking to is content where they are—they are not interested in moving. They are perfectly content with their position and how they are doing. They want to continue the conversation.

Legs standing and crossed
When you see someone standing with their legs crossed, they are actually showing open body language. This is one of the only times where body language that folds in on itself is actually positive. When you stand this way, you are actually rooting yourself in place—there's no easy way that you can move from your current position, and that shows that you are driven to remain where you are in the moment. It shows that you want to maintain the interaction that you are having at the moment without trying to cut it short.

Planting legs widely apart
When you see that legs are planted widely apart, especially when that distance is wider than shoulder-width apart, you can assume that they are aggressive. These wider stances are meant to make the individual seem larger. They do not want to mess around any longer.

Long steps
When you see someone taking longer steps around somewhere, they are showing you that they are feeling confident and in control of a situation. You can see that they are comfortable in the position that they are in.

Reading Sitting Legs in Open Positions

Sitting down can be read in very specific ways as well. We can sit in all sorts of different forms that you can identify as being necessary. Some people will sit differently than others, and this is perhaps the most pronounced when you look at the differences between male and female sitting positions. Now, this may seem surprising, but consider the fact that men and women have different hips and pelvises—women are designed to have wider pelvic regions to allow for childbirth, and that is seen in their poses. Additionally, because women tend to dress differently, wearing skirts instead of pants, you can start to identify a lot just by paying attention to how people sit.

Men sitting widely
Men tend to sit wider than women—they will sit with their legs extended naturally. However, as confidence grows, so too does the distance spread between the knees. The more widely someone spreads their legs when sitting, the more confident they feel, and the more likely that they are to keep their legs widely spread.

Women sitting with crossed legs
When you see women sitting like this, it may be that they are closed off, but, if their legs are generally relaxed, and they look comfortable, there is

likely nothing to worry about. They are probably perfectly content at the moment and will be just fine. When you look at them, they will have their legs together because they are taught to sit as such. This is to ensure that a dress is still modest enough to not flash other people.

Men using the 4 cross
Sitting in a 4 cross is sitting with one foot on the ground while the other foot is lifted up so the knee can bend with the foot on the opposite thigh. It creates a shape of a 4, which is where the name comes from. This pose is typically specific to men due to the fact that sitting this way would be revealing for women. When you see this, it is usually a sign of confidence. However, depending on how wide open it is, it could also be a form of cockiness as well.

Women stretching
Some women will sit with their legs stretched out. Typically, it is one leg stretched out over the knee or thigh of the other. Doing so makes the legs look longer, which women use to flirt. By stretching out the legs and making them look longer, women are able to show that they are interested in the other person. It is often a form of flirting and showing interest in the other person.

Feet planted on the ground
When the feet are planted firmly on the ground, it shows a neutral position in which you are trying to display that you are attentive. Women may also have just one foot planted on the ground with the other leg crossed to protect themselves from flashing other people.

Reading Standing Legs in Closed Positions
When you are closed off while standing up, your legs show this as well. Your legs will naturally be more resistant and may show that you do not want to be around the other person for any number of reasons. However, when standing, there are really only a few things that could show that.

Keeping feet close together
One thing that people do when they are closed off is to keep their feet close together. Doing this shows a degree of discomfort or even timidity. When you stand like this, you make sure that you have shrunk down—your feet closer together implies that you are standing closed off. It makes you smaller, so you are less of a target than if you stood widely.

Touching knees together
When the knees touch each other while standing, it shows nervousness. When this is done, it shows a position of shielding the genitals. This shows defensiveness, as well. It is more common in women than in men.

Taking smaller steps
When you stick to smaller, shorter steps, it usually shows that you are trying to avoid attention. You are trying to make sure that you are seen

as less aggressive. It is sometimes seen as a sort of shuffle along to try to make oneself come across as less conspicuous.

Reading Sitting Legs in Closed Positions
Closed positions when sitting are quite apparent for men, while for women, they are a bit more nuanced. You must be able to look at what the woman is doing and pay attention to her body movements. When it comes to being able to tell what people are thinking when they are sitting down, for the most part, you will be paying attention to how they sit and how close their legs are together.

Women sitting with tightly crossed legs
Women with their legs tightly crossed shows that they are usually unwilling to discuss what is happening. It is a show of lack of interest in communicating further, especially in situations where you are talking to a woman, or when there are negotiations going on.

Men sitting with crossed legs
When you see men sitting with crossed legs, it is almost always a sign of closed-off behavior. They really only sit this way when they are uncomfortable or do not really want to engage in the current discussion. Remember, showing the crotch for men is usually a show of comfort and of being assertive in the situation.

Women sitting with ankles locked around each other
When you see someone sitting with their ankles locked around each other, they are usually used to holding each other in place. You have one foot hooking around the other. This is an even more extreme version of women sitting with their legs crossed—it is an extreme form of closing yourself off and then locking yourself away.

Legs hooked onto the chair
When you see that the legs are hooking around the legs of a chair, you see signs that someone is trying to close themselves off and anchor themselves. It is a sign of restraint most of the time, typically due to nervousness or discomfort. It is an attempt to convey unwillingness.

Hugging crossed legs
When you see someone holding their legs that are crossed, as if they are almost hugging them, you are usually looking at someone who is uncomfortable. It is a complete lack of willingness to open up at all, most often when you are stuck in close proximity to people that you do not want to be around.

Holding legs against each other
When you hold your legs so the knees touch, you are showing a sign of timidity, particularly in women. It is also a habitual position sometimes as well. This is very common in women who have been taught to sit this way due to trying to prevent yourself from revealing underneath a skirt or dress.

Reading the Feet

Finally, we get to the feet. The feet are integral in making sure that you are moving along, and they provide you with lots of support as well. However, they can also reveal plenty about your mind if you know what you are looking for. When it comes to looking at the feet, you can spot willingness to go, closed off behaviors, and more.

Watching direction of feet

When you pay attention to how someone moves their feet, you can actually get a clear image of their mindset. You can see that you will actually be able to tell what they are thinking about, what's in their mind, and what they really want if you pay attention to the direction that their feet are pointing. If you want to know what they want, you simply look down at the feet. They will always tell you what it is that the person has on the mind. People will have their feet point at other people that they are interested in engaging with, or in the direction that they want to walk as if their feet are preparing themselves to go out and claim whatever it was that they wanted in the first place.

Bouncing on feet

When you see someone bounce on their feet, you watch them primarily on their toes, rolling on and off their heels. This can do one of a few things—it could show you signs that they are nervous, or that they are anxious about something. It is an attempt to eliminate and alleviate that nervous energy in hopes of being free from it.

Pacing

Pacing is a clear sign of anxiety and nervousness, especially if the individual is pacing as they speak. Think about how sometimes, people pace nervously, wringing their hands as they try to talk to someone else because they are feeling nervous. This is another way to start eliminating that restless energy.

Playing with a shoe on feet

When women in particular allow their feet to slide in and out of their shoes, they are showing signs that they are attracted to someone else. It is a clear sign of flirting when a woman does this around someone else, and it works well to attract the attention of the other person as well. Typically, this happens with the woman sitting with her legs crossed so her foot can slide in and out of the shoe in clear sight of the other person.

Shaking feet

When you see someone shaking their feet, they are usually attempting to hide a lie. This is even truer when you can see that their feet are shaking underneath a table. This is most obvious when you realize that the table that they are sitting at is also shaking with the movement, or if you can see the movements of their clothing. It is a clear sign of anxiety.

Stomping the feet
When someone stomps their feet, it is meant to show a sign of firmness. Think of how children who do not want to change up what they are doing will stomp their feet in defiance. This can additionally show aggressiveness or anger, or it could show signs of a desire for attention as well.

Tapping feet
Tapping the feet is a clear sign of tension in a situation. It is meant to show that they are actually in a position of being tense. It could also be indicative of impatience as well. The more that someone taps along their feet, the more likely that they are to show that they are done or that they want the other person to realize that they are currently uninterested in the interaction.

Touching feet
When someone touches their feet, particularly with women, they show either suggestiveness or tension. Sometimes, a gentle stroke could be seen as flirty or suggestive while trying to squeeze. It shows a sign of a need for relief from the tension.

CHAPTER 8
Proxemics

Just because body language is typically indicative of actual body movements doesn't mean that there are no other important aspects to consider as well. In particular, being able to see proxemics is an incredibly important part of being able to understand what is going on with other people. The sooner that you learn to understand and acknowledge what it is that you must do to help other people understand your position, the better, and that means taking a look at the aspects of nonverbal communication such as how someone positions themselves relative to someone else as well. Think of, for example, how someone stands and how far away they may position themselves. This is an important factor to consider because you can see a lot about how someone feels or sees the people around them by looking at where they position themselves in space as well.

Think about it—you can move around a lot in space. You can be above someone or below them. You can be near to them or far from them. This is important to acknowledge—it will help you to understand precisely what it is that is happening between people. Learning to acknowledge proxemics will help you two ways—you will be able to firstly understand people. Additionally, you will also be able to utilize proxemics your own way to influence other people around you as well. There are so many different ways that you will be able to influence others when you start making use of them.

Defining Proxemics

Proxemics is quite simple to understand: It is the positioning of someone in space around someone else. You are taking a look at how they fit into the world around them and how they choose to allow themselves to be positioned so you can then begin to recognize how everything plays out. Because of how many options that people have when it comes to putting themselves somewhere in space, there are many other ways that you can look at the situations as well. Are they gravitating toward certain people? Are they putting certain amounts of space between themselves and those around them in hopes of being able to distance themselves? This is imperative to understand: When you see how they do choose to orient themselves in approximation to other people or things, you can start piecing together a lot about intent and feelings. Someone who shies away from someone else is probably interested in being kept at a distance while someone who is trying to be closer to them may find that they are much more likely to gravitate toward them. Learning to identify those feelings matters immensely.

Within proxemics, there are two key metrics that you need to pay attention to. You must look at how someone positions themselves vertically to get a good idea of what they are thinking about the other person. This involves figuring out how to position oneself either above or below someone else. You must also take a look at horizontal proxemics as well—how far away someone tries to get from someone else. These both work in different ways and should always be read separately for the best possible results.

Vertical Space

When you read vertical space, you are taking a look at how someone positions themselves compared to everyone else around them. Some people will intentionally make themselves look taller or shorter than other people for a reason. Other times, people will intentionally get down at eye level. The best way that you can encourage the interpretation of vertical space is to take a look at eye level as a sort of axis. Eye-level is oftentimes the default level, and from there, the higher or lower someone gets will show very different meanings as well. You want to be able to read this so you can understand what to expect.

Positioning yourself above eye level

When you start above eye level, you are trying to show that you are above someone else socially as well. You are trying to assert that your own personal social standing is higher, and therefore, you get that dominance or control over a situation. Think about how people who are trying to convey just how superior they are tend to try to position themselves so that they are looking down at someone else. This can even be accomplished through simply tilting the head back, so you give the illusion of looking down your nose at someone else.

You do not have to physically be taller than someone else to be able to be in this position. You can make sure that you are sitting in a higher position than everyone else, or you can choose to simply move your head just enough that you can still look down at someone else even if you are actually shorter than them. This is important to consider—it means that even if you see that you are in a position where you are smaller than the other people, you can still make it a point to be higher up than other people.

Of course, this is reserved for trying to look down on someone in the literal and metaphorical sense—you are making it clear that you are above them or that they are beneath you because you do not want to deal with them. This is usually rude, condescending, or even aggressive, depending on the context. It has a lot to do with intimidation attempts. It can be a boss trying to demand that someone else does something for them, positioning themselves higher up in a taller chair. It could be someone looking down their nose at you. No matter what, however, being above eye level typically comes with the connotations of trying to belittle or demean the other person.

Positioning yourself below eye level
When you position yourself below eye level, you do something different—you make yourself submissive or less threatening. It usually betrays a distinct lack of confidence in a situation and is a sign that someone is trying to make themselves smaller. It is usually seen with people who are shy, in trouble, or otherwise trying to make themselves less conspicuous. Below eye level is a sign that someone is trying to make it a point to make themselves smaller so they can stay out of sight. It also has a tendency to make someone feel inferior, as well.

Think of the effect that adults have on children when they are trying to scold them. Children usually feel frightened or intimidated by virtue of the fact that they are lower than the adult. This can happen to adults as well—they are intimidated by the appearance that they are less superior to others. This is an inherently unconfident, uncomfortable position, and that is precisely why people are told to keep their heads held highly when it comes to being able to boost confidence—sitting up with high heads actually helps with it.

Positioning yourself at eye level
When you position yourself at eye level, you are setting yourself up on even footing. By making sure that you are both on the same eye level, you will be able to make it clear to the other person that you value them as an equal. It shows respect and tact with the other person—it shows that you are not trying to dominate or threaten them and that they can expect you to be kind or understanding.

There are several different times where it is imperative that you put yourself at eye level if you are taller. This is precisely why, in business meetings, everyone's chairs adjust—it allows for everyone to be at eye level with each other. It is also why people are told to get down to the level of the children to talk to them as well. It is a highly important thing to remember—you can position yourself at the same level so you can show that openness to other people. This is the only level that is truly open on both sides of the interaction.

Horizontal Space
You must also consider the usage of the horizontal space around you as well. It is the distance that you want to put between yourself and other people. We naturally position ourselves closer to people that we trust or are close to emotionally, and we distance ourselves from strangers. This happens consistently, and when you cannot naturally position yourself as further away, you will make it a point to refuse to acknowledge the other person. This is why people can sit touching strangers on a bus or train without feeling distressed—they simply pretend that the other person is not there and ignore them to the best of their ability.

When you want to take a look at the distance that people hold themselves apart from others, you will see that there are primarily four different distances to look for. You can see people that position themselves closely together, choosing to do so within inches or feet while others choose to distance themselves significantly. Usually speaking, you will see that people will naturally fall into these patterns, and they are very predictable. This is why you can tell the difference between a couple that has clearly been together for a while and a couple of strangers. It's easy to spot that familiarity between people at a glance, and a major part of that is in looking at the horizontal space that they are maintaining between each other.

Positioning yourself in the intimate zone
The first of the positions that you can be in when considering the distances between people is the intimate zone. The intimate zone is the closest to positions. It is reserved for those that are the closest to you. It is those that are lovers, partners, or closest friends. Very few people are actually allowed to get this close to you. Generally, young children also get that option to be in the intimate zone for a period of time as well, usually until they start aging and deciding that they want their freedom. This is within just about one foot of the individual. It could also be touching as well, or anything in between.

When you are forced into this zone with someone that is not close enough to be within this space, you will typically distance yourself from them—you will engage in what is known as depersonalization. When you do this, you will intentionally make yourself stop thinking or feeling about the person as a person. You depersonalize them—you try to make it less comfortable for yourself by entirely ignoring the other person so that you can feel better about the situation.

Positioning yourself in the personal zone
When it comes to the personal zone, you are looking at friends and family members that are a bit more distant from you. It may be people that you know somewhat well, but would not be comfortable getting involved with on closer terms. When it comes to friends and family, you will generally allow some to get closer to others. Usually, the ones that are allowed to be closer to others are those that are closer friends. You may stand with a best friend much closer than to someone that you do not know very well. Your acquaintances will be kept further in the personal zone while your siblings or parents are probably much closer within this range.

The personal zone ranges between 1.5 and 5 feet of the other person. It is an important space to recognize. In this zone, you will sort of shift out who is closer and further to you. Most of the time, you will see that those closer together tend to like each other or be closer to each other than those that are further.

Positioning yourself in the social zone
When you position yourself in the social zone, you are putting yourself at a comfortable distance in which you would have no problems allowing

other people to pass you by, even if you did not know them. Usually, you will allow yourself to be far enough away from people that you are unsure about. This is so you are not getting in their personal space, and they are not bothering you either. In this zone, you could ignore people without a problem, or you could choose to interact still without having to approach any closer.

Between 5 and 15 feet make up the social zone. This is the distance that allows for the most flexibility in terms of the interactions that you will have. When you keep people in this zone, you are able to avoid strangers or other people that you simply do not care to engage with.

Positioning yourself in the public zone

Finally, the public zone is a functional space at which you are far enough away that you can directly influence or interact with other people while a crowd of people can see you at the same time. This is the position where you try to keep yourself when you are trying to address several other people at any given point in time. By entering the public zone, you are interacting with people in a way that allows for you to be listened to. You position yourself roughly 12 feet away or further. Now that we have the creation of technology that will help with the projection of voice and image, the public zone can grow to be much larger as well. Think about it—you can be in the social zone even when you are thousands of feet away now in a stadium just due to the fact that your voice and image can still be projected for everyone else to see and hear.

CHAPTER 9
Haptics

The last form of nonverbal communication that we are going to address is that of haptics. Haptics makes up the ability that you have to communicate with other people via touch. It is a very important method to consider, especially due to the fact that touch can vary so much from person to person. Some touches are meant to convey happiness, comfort, or pleasantries. Other touches are meant to be hurtful. Others still are supposed to get attention from others, and there are still other types of hugs and touches that convey a desire to be closer or more intimate. All of this is important—it is good to be able to see the different ways that people touch each other. When you look at the different kinds of touches, you can start to identify the different kinds of relationships that people have with each other. Some people will touch in certain areas that have certain functional meanings. This is what haptics is—the communication made through touch.

Functional Touch
Functional touch is the first kind of touch to consider. These are impersonal forms of touching that are not meant to do anything one way or another. When you are looking at functional touches, you are considering the various different kinds of touches that are meant to be able to convey a purposeful meaning. They are the most commonly associated with different kinds of touches that are supposed to be used in professional kinds of settings. The more that you see this sort of touch play out, the more you realize that they are designed to simply convey respectful acknowledgment. Think of a handshake before negotiations—that is a form of functional touching. Additionally, a pat on the shoulder would be deemed functional as well.

This sort of functional touch is usually initiated by the dominant individual. It is okay for a dominant member of a party to initiate this kind of touching over someone that is less dominant. However, it is usually much less socially acceptable for someone else to instigate. It is not as acceptable for someone to touch their manager or boss as it would be for their manager to pat them on the shoulder.

Social Touch
Social touch is another important aspect that you must consider. When you look at the social touch, you are considering the different ways that you look at how people engage with those that they are close to. Usually, social touch is used by people attempting to touch those that they are engaging with on a more personal level. When you consider how people tend to engage with each other socially, you see non-vulnerable touching—touches that are limited. To certain areas that are not deemed

intimate enough to be positioned anywhere else. When you see social touches, you see touches that are meant to be on the arm, hand, or shoulder. They are touches that do not immediately lead to you backing away from the other person. These sorts of touches are meant to be acceptable from even strangers.

Typically touches here are meant to redirect attention. For example, consider someone that is trying to get attention from someone else. For example, consider that someone just tapped on your shoulder to get your attention. This is a normal way for you to get someone else's attention that would not be considered too personal.

Friendship Touch

When you look at friendship touches, you are considering those that are designed to be friendly without actually instigating anything. Think of the way that you would touch a good friend of yours. You are not trying to be romantic or intimate with them—you are showing a platonic friendliness, and that friendliness should go far. When you are interacting with people who use platonic friendship touches, you will mostly notice that they happen between women. Men typically see these sorts of touches as an attempt to dominate instead of an attempt to get things right.

Friendship touches are reserved, then, for those that are actually somewhat close to each other. This can start to push past those points of closed-off areas, such as the waist or the lower back. When you are friendly with someone, you start to feel like you are okay, pushing past those boundaries a bit more often. This is essential—when you do this more, you are able to better build that closeness with people that will take you far.

Intimate Touch

When you look at intimate touch, you are pushing the touches past that friendship place. When you think of this, you can start to blur that line between romantic and friendship—they may happen in relationships that are not romantic, but, often, they are found within them. These are touches that are usually more likely to be seen as public displays of affection. You might see, for example, that you are hugging the other person, or that you are holding hands. This implies that the relationship is much closer than it otherwise would be. When you take a look at these sorts of relationships, you will be identifying general closeness between people.

Sexual Touch

Finally, when you consider the sexual touch of people, you will see that they are meant to be the most intimate. This is primarily reserved for lovers and partners and is designed as the most comfortable zone that you can be in. It is meant to establish love through intimacy. In general, you will see that though it is physically intimate, physical intercourse may not actually be the end goal. Sexual touches also include nuzzling up against a spouse, hugging them, kissing them, or touching them in a way that is primarily reserved for someone that you are going to be intimate with romantically.

CHAPTER 10
Identifying Body Language Clusters

Now, at this point, we have spent time looking over all sorts of situations in which you are able to understand how people are thinking. You have now seen several different ways that you need to read the other people in your life. From being able to see how people engage with each other and with you, you can start to figure out what it is that they want, what they like, and what they need. Being able to spot if someone is open or closed is perfect when it comes to trying to figure out just what it is that they are thinking or feeling. When you do this, you will be able to see just what it is that you need to understand. You will be able to see when you should be thinking about what the other person is trying to do. However, you need more than just understanding that certain movements usually mean one thing or another—you need to look at the clusters of body language as well. If you want to be able to understand what it is that is being conveyed properly; you must be able to also see the clusters of body language.

Remember, body language and nonverbal communication usually comes in clusters. It comes in groups that directly convey whatever it is that you are trying to say. Think about it: You could, for example, be lying to someone else only to realize that your body language is directly conveying that point. When you see that other people's body language comes into these clusters, then you can start looking for them.

Of course, those clusters of body language can vary greatly from cluster to cluster. For this reason, we are going to go through several common clusters of body language so you can start to understand what they all are. Some movements, as we have determined thus far, will have very specific meanings that you will have to keep in mind. When you consider these clusters, you should have an easier time starting to understand them.

Body Language of Dominance

Let's begin with the body language of dominance. This is a very particular type of body language that you can identify almost immediately if you know what you are looking for. Ultimately, the way that you can identify dominance is by making sure that you pay attention to posture, expressions, and also general demeanor. We'll go over three key points here: Creating dominant postures, creating dominant expressions, and fostering that sense of general dominance.

Most of the time, when you see someone in a dominant posture, you will see that they are wide open. You are looking at someone that is creating expansive, wide body language that is supposed to be confident. Dominance is often a form of confidence that is then made stronger or more assertive. It is making it clear that you are confident in your position and that your position is over someone else—you are asserting that you are in charge. There is a fine line between dominance and aggression that must be managed as well. You will need to pay close attention to this point and keep it in mind.

Dominant body language will require you to expand your body. You want to make yourself bigger than the other person—not necessarily literally, but spatially. When you do this, you are looking for ways that you can expand your body language, such as standing up taller, holding your head straighter, or even just trying to make yourself seem wider by standing with your arms and legs further apart.

As you walk about, you would expect to show signs of dominance as well—primarily, you would want to ensure that you are showing that you take wider steps. Remember, wideness is usually going to go hand in hand with confidence and dominance as well. If you want to make it clear that you are dominant, you will also need to make sure that you have the right expression as well.

Dominant expressions are usually those that are primarily neutral. The more unenthusiastic that you look, the better because that lack of enthusiasm appears disinterested and therefore, unimpressed. By having that unimpressed façade, you will see that you are actually in complete control over the situation. When you look at others with that disinterest, they will start to feel unnerved, granting the dominance that you were looking for.

Additionally, you will want to make sure that you make good use of eye contact as well. You want to make sure that you are maintaining proper eye contact at all times to ensure that you are actually showing the dominance that you need. If you want to make sure that you do your job and show that dominance off, you must make sure that you start with eye contact. Dominant individuals will make their eye contact long, even almost uncomfortably so, and they smile less as well. You will also see signs that the other person will avoid eye contact entirely sometimes as well—this is done intentionally to make it clear that the other person is not worth the time.

The most common body language that you can expect to see with dominant individuals, then, includes the following:

- **Hands positioned on the hips:** When you position your hands on your hips, you will find that you are positioned in such a way that you will be able to show your own assertiveness. Remember, hands on the hips are often positioned this way because they are meant to be at the ready—but it is commonly mistaken as an attempt to be dominant. Because of that, it is quite effective at showing that you are in control of a situation.
- **Showing off the crotch (for men):** Men, in particular, will utilize the quintessential crotch display when they are trying to make themselves dominant. Men will intentionally hold their

hands to their crotch to point out their crotches. This is done to try to say that their crotch is bigger, and therefore, they are more dominant.
- **Utilizing hair:** Some people, male and female, will intentionally use their hair to make themselves taller. They will intentionally style their hair so they have it higher up on their heads, therefore, making them a bit taller than they would be otherwise.
- **Utilizing touch:** Remember, in professional settings, you want to avoid touching people that are more dominant than you are. You want to make sure that you are putting yourself in a position where the more dominant individuals are able to be more above the others in context. This means that if you are the one that initiates the touching, you will be more in control of the situation and therefore, more dominant.
- **Walking in the middle of a path:** When you position yourself in the middle of a path, you force other people to have to move for you. You make it so that they will have no choice but to move over to let you through. This utter command of the space that you have makes it clear that you've got the position that you are in for a reason.
- **Wearing high heels (for women):** Some women will intentionally wear heels that will make themselves taller. Again, this allows for the creation of being taller. It is done to try to make the individual more capable of standing over others so that they can assert their dominance.

Body Language of Attraction

Now, let's take a moment to consider the body language of attraction. When you take a look at attraction, you can usually spot it almost immediately. Attracted body language is clear as day—it shows clear cut signs of being present just due to the fact that the individual is trying to make you see it. When someone is attracted to the other person, most of the time, they want the other person to take notice so they can determine whether it is reciprocated or not. When you want to take a look at this kind of body language, you will be looking for some unconscious signs that the other person's body is responding to you.

Of course, attraction has to be divided into male and female—the two sexes show vastly different signs that they are interested in someone else. Men usually are easier to read than women when it comes to identifying that attraction, and that means that you can usually tell at a glance how they are doing. If you want to ensure that you accurately identify what is going on with someone else, you will be taking a look at a few key signs. For men, these include:

- **Checking you out:** When he is attracted to you, he will check you out—and he won't be as discreet about it. He will be trying to show you that he is interested and that he wants to make it a point to see more of you. This is important to him—he wants you to know that he considers you an option in case you may also consider him one as well.

- **Face touching:** Men who are attracted to someone else will also touch their faces more often. This could be in the ears, chin, cheeks, or anywhere else. It is part of nervousness, part grooming, and part sexual flirtation. People who are turned on by someone else tend to be more touchy with themselves due to their sensitive skin.
- **Flashing the eyebrows:** When you see that someone has flashed their eyebrows, they raise their eyes just slightly, and it is brief. It typically is a subtle sign, but it allows for more to be seen of the individual. This shows attraction is showing an attempt to widen the visual field because they like the other person. It also allows the other person to see more of their own eyes, which is key.
- **Grooming:** There are a multitude of different grooming behaviors that men who are attracted to someone else will show as well. IN particular, they may attempt to fix their hair or make sure that their clothes are just right. They want to look their best for those that they are attracted to. They may also make it a point to mess with buttons or fix their socks.
- **He touches you:** He will also make it a point to touch you while trying to explain it away as accidental. He doesn't want you to think that it is intentional, but he also wants you to know that he is interested, or trigger you to be interested in him as well. Additionally, he may plant his hand on your back as well, guiding you around and showing to others that he has already started to claim you.
- **Moving more often:** Men who are around someone that they are attracted to will naturally move around more. They will fiddle with things, run hands through their hair, or otherwise attempt to move around, hoping to pull the attention of the person that they are trying to attract to them.
- **Opening the face:** For men, when they are attracted to someone else, they open their faces. This is several different movements at the same time. They will show flared nostrils with raising their brows and parting their lips. This all works together to create an inviting look while also signaling that they are comfortable and interested in continuing to engage with that individual.
- **Parting the lips:** When men see someone that they are attracted to, usually, their lips will part briefly as soon as eye contact is

made. This is a clear sign of attraction, and you will be able to tell more if you can see the tongue moving slightly as well.
- **Raising brows when listening:** Men, when they are listening to someone that they are attracted to, will focus intently on what is being said. They will also make it a point to raise their eyebrows slightly, opening the face-up. This also serves to allow him to see more of you all in one go as well.
- **The crotch display:** Just as with dominance, you are likely to see the crotch display in attraction. When men point or emphasize their crotches, they want you to pay attention there so that they can get your attraction as well.

Women, when they are attracted to someone, tend to be a bit more subtle. They create simpler cues that are able to be picked up if you know what you are looking for. They include movements such as:

- **Eye contact:** Women make a very specific type of eye contact with someone when they are attracted to them. Usually, it is displayed by looking up at the person, then looking down at the lips before going right back to eye contact. The eye contact is usually through her lashes—she often tilts her head just right, so she has to look up at him.
- **Foot play:** Women will often play with their feet when they are attracted to someone, sitting cross-legged just long enough to be able to show off her legs to win you over.
- **Higher rates of blinking:** When some women blink regularly, they find themselves blinking far more often than they otherwise would have been. This is readily apparent if you pay attention. She will blink more often, and usually, her head will be tilted as well. She is batting her eyes at you in hopes of attracting you.
- **Playing with hair:** When she plays with her hair, whether twirling it around her fingers, tossing it over her shoulder, or otherwise, what she is doing is making it a point to show you that she is attracted. She shows off her neck and also pushes pheromones into the air.
- **She blushes:** You may notice that she finds herself blushing more often when you look at her—she can't help it! This is good—it is a sign that you're making her heart rate pick up and making her interested in you.
- **She displays her chest more:** Women tend to shift into a pose where they are standing with an arched back. By doing this, they push out their breasts and therefore, make them draw more attention. They may also push out their bottoms as well in hopes of making themselves more attractive to the individual. It is an attempt to display the body with hopes of the other person finding it attractive.

- **She gives you a seductive look:** The seductive look is what everyone constantly calls the bedroom eyes—it is looking at the other person with that look of longing and desire.
- **She laughs at everything you say, even if it is not funny:** Often, you will see that women who are attracted to someone think that they are the funniest person around. They can't stop laughing at them and will continue to find them entirely entertaining.
- **She leans in:** Women who lean into the other person are trying to get them to notice their attraction. She will make it a point to lean into you in hopes that she will be able to attract you and win you over.
- **She tries to attract you to her lips:** Often, women will make it a point to draw attention to their lips when they are attracted to someone. If she is on a date with you, she may make it a point to show you that her lips are there simply by wearing lipstick or trying to draw more attention to them by parting them.
- **The breathing rate:** She may not realize it, but her breathing will pick up in intensity and speed just slightly when she is around someone that she is attracted to. This is done because of the fact that attraction boosts the heart rate, which then increases the breathing rate. You can see this in particular if you were to take the time to look at her shoulders to pay attention to the breathing rate that she is showing you.

Body Language of Confidence

The body language of confidence is highly important—when you have the right, confident body language, you will find that everything else is so much easier to cope with. Ultimately, the way that you can get through having the right kind of body language is by making sure that you are able to interact with other people better. Having that proper confidence is essential if you want to be able to work well with others. If you are able to create a confident air to yourself, you would find that you can actually begin to be much more successful.

The truth is, being able to be confident is essential. If you cannot manage to maintain that essential confidence and that willingness to be out there and trust yourself, you are going to struggle. Confidence matters, especially if you are trying to interview for a job or otherwise need to make yourself assertive. Just being able to put yourself out there and show that you can and will be a confident person is often enough. However, that requires you to build up confidence in the first place.

The good news is, confident body language is often created simply through sheer confidence in general. If you want to make it clear that you are confident in the moment, you will want to make sure that you are paying better attention to everyone else. You want to ensure that you are able to create that degree of confidence that you will need, and you do that simply by starting to fake it. Yes—if you want to be confident, the best way to do so is simply through trying to pretend to be confident in the first place.

It all begins with having the right confident expression. To begin, you must make it a point to start with eye contact. The best way to be confident is to start with having the right degree of eye contact to ensure that you come across as comfortable. This is difficult to get just right, but confident individuals tend to use eye contact that follows the ratio of making eye contact 50% of the time during speaking and 70% of the time when listening to what someone else has to say. If you can follow this rule, you can usually ensure that you are on the right track. Additionally, you must make sure that you smile as well. Genuine smiles will help to show confidence, especially when paired up with the eye contact that you want to make.

If you want to get the right posture, then you will want to take a look at trying to create a welcoming position. This means that you want to balance being open and relaxed with confidence at the same time. This is because ideally, you should not be concerned about what other people are doing. You should not be afraid of what they will say or do, and you should be able to naturally allow your body language to expand outward. The more that you do this, the more likely that you are to find that you do feel more confident.

Most confident posture has a few key points to remember:

- **Stand up straight and tall:** Keeping your posture up tall will help you to be seen as confident more often. It will help you to be seen as someone that is in control of the situation. However, you want to be tall without looking down at the other person, which is reserved for being seen as dominant instead of just confident.
- **Stand comfortably:** You must also make sure that you are simply comfortable. If you are standing stiffly, it will become clear that you are standing in a way that will show that you are not confident or comfortable given the current situation that you are in. You must make sure that you pay attention to the positions that you use.
- **Keep hands visible:** Perhaps one of the easiest things that you can do to make yourself be seen as confident is to make sure that you stand up with your hands visible. Making sure that you keep your hands helps you to ensure that you are positioning yourself in a way that shows that you are not trying to hide them. In fact, you may even choose to talk with your hands, utilizing them to show that you do like what you are doing.
- **Show that you are listening:** When you make sure that you show that you are listening to the other person, you are seen as

confident. You are not concerning yourself with trying to pay attention to other aspects of what is going on.

Body Language of Insecurity

Insecurity is a type of body language that you will need to get to know. When you learn to read insecurity, you will start to see what it is that is on their minds. Usually, insecurity is visible when you consider the ways that someone engages with other people, and it is very important to understand it—when you know that someone is showing signs of insecurity, you can start to see that they have very clear problems. You will see that they are struggling and that you may need to offer comfort or help in some way to try to better the situation.

We all feel insecure at different points in time, and that is the most obvious when you take a look at body language. You might find that you are playing more with your hair or biting your nails. You may also attempt to play with items that will help you to displace energy. All of this is pretty typical, but you need to understand that they cause problems. They make you seem much less confident, and that can be a problem. If you appear nervous at a job interview, for example, you might come across as struggling to show your own degree of confidence. You make it clear that you are not actually trusting yourself, and that can be a major problem.

When you see someone showing that they are insecure, you will immediately be able to tell just due to the fact that their body language will be more closed off. They shrink inward instead of attempting to communicate outward. They will be unwilling to listen to other people due to their own stubbornness, or they may also cause problems because they pull away from others.

A common sign of insecurity is the creation of barriers between oneself and those around them. They want to make sure that the other people see that they are actively attempting to shield themselves. They want to ensure that their ability to shield themselves is actually heeded and that the other people will leave them alone. The most common creation of a barrier happens with arms. If arms are not crossed, then the hands may be shoved in the pockets instead.

Another telltale sign is to position oneself so that you are oriented away from the other person. You may find that you stick yourself in directions that show that you are not going to face the other person. You stand at an angle to try to prevent yourself from being directly faced as well. In seated positions, you might find your feet moving nervously. You may also see that they are hooked around the legs of the chair as well. It is possible that you will try to root yourself to your chair to be closed off.

When you are insecure, there are obvious signs in the face as well—you are likely to stand with little eye contact with the other person. You are too nervous to actually make it, so you try to avert your gaze as much as possible. Your brows are probably lowered as well in an attempt to shield your eyes because you do not want that direct eye contact with the other person. Additionally, you may chew on or lick your lips. This is not done in attraction here—it is because your lips are drying out due to your nervousness. The chin also tucks inward during nervousness and insecurity to make yourself smaller and less imposing to those around you.

CHAPTER 11
Using Body Language

Finally, we are at the end of the book. Now, it is time to be able to look at body language itself and how it tends to create influential behaviors for people. We are going to see just how you can begin to influence other people to create exactly what you are looking for. If you know what you are doing, you can actually heavily influence the way that other people interact. With the use of your own body language, you can begin to create all sorts of situations and expectations.

For example, consider that you want to influence someone so that they do what you want to do. If you know what you are doing, you will be able to change up how they tend to engage. Your confidence, for example, could influence someone else so that they will make it a point to change up what they are doing. Confidence sells. Or, if you want to get someone to stop doing something, you can assert that as well. There are also ways that you can position yourself to be deemed dominant over other people, something that is highly powerful as well. If you do this, you can start to recognize that you are capable of that influence.

Of course, if you know how to influence other people, you will need to be mindful of why you do so or how you decide to. When you want to influence other people, you must do so in a way that will help you—you want to make sure that you do so in such a way that is mindful of what other people are dealing with. You must ensure that you are actively making it a point to create that body language that you need in a situation, while also balancing out your expectations that you have for the other person as well. You should not just decide that you are going to force someone to do something to your own benefit.

Within this chapter, we are going to explore a few different concepts—we will be looking at the concept of neuro-linguistic programming, which heavily utilizes body language so that you can influence other people. From there, we will take the time to go over what you can do to begin changing your own body language. We will go over how you can change up what you are doing so that you are showing them what it is that you should be doing. Finally, we will explain several different uses for your own body language that will create the effects that you are looking for. As you learn to utilize this, you will get better at being able to control everything that you need.

Introducing the Concept of Neuro-Linguistic Programming

Neuro-linguistic programming, also commonly known as NLP, is designed to create the effect of influencing the behaviors of someone else just by making use of the way that you move or speak yourself. NLP takes control of your nonverbal communication that you use and then utilizes your own movements to influence the unconscious mind of the other person.

Think about it—when you utilize NLP, you are going to be changing up your body language so that you can get the other person to do what you want. You can change up your body language to influence them to say yes to something, for example, or you can mirror them to make them like you more to allow yourself to better influence them as well. NLP works as a way that you can essentially control the other person without having to do a thing. Through being able to make these differences in your own behaviors, you will see that you can actually control other people, and that is highly powerful and compelling as well. If you keep it up, you can begin to make more use of it. You can ensure that you are on the right track when it comes to influencing other people.

NLP was designed originally to grant average people who know little about psychology the training that they would need to control themselves. When you utilize NLP, you are able to begin controlling yourself and those around you. Consider this—you are trying to become more confident. However, the more that you try, the less that you do because you are stuck. You find yourself completely caught up with the negativity that you feel, and you never actually improve your behaviors. As this happens more and more often, you will begin to see that your own negative thoughts get worse. However, with NLP, you can start to influence them. You can start to change up those thoughts to grant yourself that ability to better change your mindset as well to create positivity instead. This can be done through all sorts of different possible options. If you're interested, you may want to check out a book dedicated to NLP—there are many of them, and you can find that there is a lot more to it other than simply utilizing unconscious behaviors to control thoughts and feelings.

Changing Your Own Body Language

If you want to be able to influence the behaviors of other people, the best starting point is in making sure that you look at how to identify your body language when looking at how it plays out in regards to others as well. If you want to be able to have that confident body language, you must first learn those steps to ensure that you change up the body language in the first place. Thankfully, changing your own body language is not as hard as you probably think—you can actually do so relatively easily.

With just a few steps, you can start to change up your own body language. With just a few simple changes toward how you approach your situation and what you do, you will be able to see that you have far more power than you gave yourself credit for. It won't take you much—you just have to try. It will get easier over time—you will become fully capable of figuring out what you need to do and how to do it. You will be able to do it at will after enough time, and that will be powerful.

Step 1: Start with identifying your body language as it is
First, you will begin by checking on your current body language. What are you doing in the moment? How are you feeling as you sit there? What is it that your body language is currently conveying? Is it positive or negative? Is it related to what you want it to be? Would you rather find a way that you can communicate something different? The beginning point is making sure that you know what you are doing so you can then make the changes over time. Start out with this idea of what you are doing in the moment so you can move on to the next step.

Step 2: Think about what you want to convey
From there, it is time to figure out what it is that you are trying to convey to the other party. Figure out what it is that you want to convey to the other person. Do you want to be happy? Frustrated? Annoyed? Figure that out and make note of it. That is the next big thing: You must make sure that you change up your body language to ensure that you are on track. When you know what it is that you want to convey, you can then move on to the next level.

Step 3: Begin altering the expression
Step 3 helps you to begin making it clear what you are trying to convey. You will begin to assume the expression of what it is that you are trying to get across to the other person. If you are trying to be confident with them, then you would attempt to assume that expression. If you are trying to be dominant, you would take on a dominant expression, and if you wanted to attract someone, you would show them that as well.

Step 4: Alter the posture
Once you've got the expression down, you start changing up your pose as well. You would begin to take on the right posture to show that you are, in fact, confident in the behaviors that you are attempting to create. The posture will help you to begin to alter the way that other people see you.

Step 5: Practice
Finally, you must make sure that you get better. Being able to change up your behaviors so that you can then influence other people takes serious practice—it is not exactly easy to just wake up one day and decide that you are going to start changing up how you behave. You will have to take the time to get to know the people around you. You must learn through experience that it is something that you can do in the first place.

Using Body Language

When it comes to mastering the use of body language, you must make it a point to utilize the different types of emotions that you want to convey. It does take practice, but, over time, you will find that it is actually somewhat easy to do when you can master it. We are going to go over several different ways that you can begin to utilize body language to create the different effects that you are looking for. The sooner that you learn these, the sooner you realize that you can do better.

Mirroring

Before you begin any sort of influential movements to other people, you must make sure that you have the rapport to do so. You must ensure that you are on the right page to ensure that you are on track to ensuring that they are better capable of following along with you. You will need to ensure that you choose out behaviors that you know will be helpful for you. If you want to make sure that you are able to influence others, then you start out learning to mirror. As you develop rapport, you get better at also influencing other people. Thankfully, this is a simple process—you just have to know where to start.

To begin, all you have to do is start feeling like you do have a connection with the other person. When you do this, you begin to build up that relationship between you both. Take some time feeling like you are genuinely connected to the other person. Then, when you feel that connection, it is time to start using it.

You don't want to start out with simply changing your body language to match theirs—this can be too apparent if you are not very familiar with the other person. But, what you can do is match another aspect of their body language. You can choose to match their vocal cues instead. By doing so, you create the same effect, but it is harder to catch on that you are being copied if you are only being copied in mannerisms of speech. In particular, you will want to make sure that you match volume, speed, and fervor of speaking.

Then, with that match, you need to identify the punctuator that the other person is using. This is what they use to create a major sort of influence on what they are doing. You will want to watch how they talk. When they say something that they want to emphasize, they will do something. There will be some sort of mark. They might, for example, make it a point to raise their eyebrows, or they might move their hands a certain way. When you figure out what it is that they do, you can then utilize it. In order to mirror them, then you must make use of their punctuator so you can convince them that you do understand them. The next time that you sense that they would use their punctuator, you make it a point to do so instead. They then get the sense that you know them far better and that you understand them. This allows the creation of rapport.

To determine if you have succeeded, all you have to do is make it a point to move and see if they copy you. Do they move along with you? If they do, then they have picked up on your change in behavior, and they've chosen to adopt it as well. This is perfect for you—it means that they will be more receptive to everything that you do.

Nodding for influence

One way that you can begin to influence other people is simply by making it a point to nod your head when you ask a question. Did you know that through simply nodding your head, you can influence the other person to start to feel compelled to say yes to you? This is commonly used by people trying to practice NLP, and it can be used easily.

To begin, you will want to make sure that you are on good terms with the other person. This is commonly done through mirroring, but if you have a good relationship already, you can make use of this easily. For example, imagine that you want to ask your partner or spouse to do something. You would get their attention, and you'd want to make sure that they were looking at you. Then, as you make eye contact, you can start to nod your head to them. You can start making it clear that you are interested in asking them something. Then, you will want to nod your head, but the catch here is that you cannot be conspicuous about it. They cannot know what you are doing, or you will find yourself making it less likely that you would be able to get them to agree to what you are asking.

As you nod your head, you should do so barely perceptibly. This will influence them to start nodding their head slightly as well. This is because we naturally mirror those that we are close to. If you are close to your partner, you will find that they will copy you naturally, and you will then be able to make use of their natural inclination to follow your pace.

When they start nodding their head as you ask the question, you put them into the right mindset to say yes to you. You put them into that mindset that you can utilize to ensure that you do get what you want.

Positioning yourself as dominant

Another trick that you can use your body language for is to make yourself seem more dominant to the other person. When you are able to position yourself just right, you can actually win negotiations much easier just by virtue of the fact that you will be able to shift your behaviors. For example, many CEOs will position themselves just the right way to ensure that they are dominant in just about any situation. They will make it so that their chair is higher and then place a chair that does not have adjustable settings across from them. In doing so, they create a situation in which the other person is naturally underneath them. This allows their dominance to be asserted naturally, even if they were shorter and without having to do anything much at all to make it happen. Just by virtue of positioning them at a different level, you will see a big change.

Dominant body language can also be used to expand out around other people—you can choose to make yourself wider, more likely to extend yourself, or otherwise just by virtue of pushing yourself out wider. Take up more space at a meeting at the table, and you will naturally be seen as more dominant. Make people wait for you or otherwise utilize wider steps to show that you are bigger than the other person. This will naturally allow you to begin changing up the mindset that the other person has without them even realizing it. Just by virtue of being able to do this, you should be able to see that they will change up how they approach the situation as well.

Setting the pace

You can also utilize what is known as setting the pace to allow yourself to be more capable of influencing a mindset that the other person may have as well. One such way to do this is to first match the pace of the other person. This could be a literal pace in walking—you would simply step along with the other person. You'd make sure that you were lined up just right to start matching them from the beginning. Or, if they are tapping on the table, you could match their tapping. Essentially, you begin by mirroring the other person first. You want to make sure that you are following along with their behaviors before you then try to change them. In matching their pace, you do something very important with your own body language. You tell their unconscious mind that you are on good terms with them. You are showing what is known as rapport—essentially meaning that your relationship is good.

Then, as you continue to match their pace, you can start to alter it. You can start slowing down in a literal sense if you are walking alongside them. By making sure that you are walking at the same pace, you can make sure that you are both moving the same way. The hope is, as you do this, you will watch them continue to match pace with you. They will naturally change up their own body language to ensure that they are on the same page. They will naturally take the same pace as you just by virtue of the fact that they believe that the rapport is already there.

By doing this, you get control over some basic actions that can actually have massive changes to the body language of the other person. You can get them to relax or stop doing something nervously if you know what you are doing. You can get people to match your speed, or you can convince them that they need to change up what they are doing in other situations as well. The more that you work on how to do this, the better off you will be. This is a very important skill to develop if you want to make sure that you get those good influences.

CONCLUSION

And with that, you've arrived at the end of the book! You now know everything that you would need for a cursory understanding of what you need to do if you want to analyze other people. Being able to analyze others is highly powerful. It is influential, and it will help you to navigate the world better—the more that you learn to read other people and understand them, the easier it becomes for you to get through everything. As you become more skilled at being able to make those choices that you need, you will discover that you can actually do far better. You can start to come up with all the ways that you can better engage with people. You will be able to begin working better with people all around you.

The ability to read other people is powerful. It will help you to become more confident in yourself, and it can also help you to influence other people. You can use it to avoid being lied to or get along with people better. No matter the purpose, however, you now have the skills that you would need to ensure that you are on the right track. You now have the skills that you would need if you wanted to ensure that you could do more.

Remember, with this kind of power, you can begin to influence other people with ease. You can begin to change up what they do, how they do it, and why. However, with that skill, you must also acknowledge that you need to do so in a positive manner. You must acknowledge that you need to do better so that you can properly engage well with those around you. By learning to master this fact, accepting that you need to be responsible for what you do with this power, you will realize that you have far more options than you thought possible.

And now, as this book comes to a close, it is time for you to start considering what you will do, how you will do it, and why. It is time for you to start figuring out what you want to do. It is time to begin putting the information that you have learned here to good use. How do you choose to use it? Will you allow yourself to become more confident? Will you allow yourself to step back? Will you step forward? What will you do to ensure that you are on track with what you want, your goals, and how you want to live life? This book provided you with the tools that you would need, but now it is up to you to master them. It is up to you to figure out what you will need to do if you want to be able to become someone that is more confident, more aware of what you are doing, and more able to be certain that you are ready to succeed.

Thank you for taking the time to read through this book. Hopefully, as you did read through this book, you found that it was filled up with all sorts of important information that you can use for yourself. Hopefully, you feel much more confident in your ability to navigate social situations, and hopefully, you feel ready to take on the world. At this point, what you do next is entirely up to you! You can take it all on, or you can choose to allow the knowledge to go unused. No matter what, however, if you found that this book has helped you in your goals, please consider heading to Amazon to leave a review! Your feedback is always greatly appreciated!

DESCRIPTION

Are you sick of trying to understand other people, only to feel like you are completely and utterly lost? Are you done with constantly misunderstanding what people are trying to convey to you because you can't seem to understand the most basic of body language when you try to? If so, then keep reading... this book is for you.

Being able to understand the body language of other people is highly important—being able to see what it is that people want or need in a situation is great—it helps you to figure out what it is that you will need. It helps you to understand that ultimately, they are trying to communicate something to you. Especially because of the fact that your unconscious mind controls your body language and your actions in general, you want to be able to see what it is that drives people to do what they do. Through watching body language, you can tell the difference between people who are wide open with each other and people who are not. You can see the difference between being willing to engage with someone and being afraid of the people around you.

These skills are highly beneficial to you. They can help you when it comes to being able to negotiate. They can teach you how you will be able to better get what you want. You will be able to interview better, to avoid being lied to, and to attract more people simply because you will know that you understand their thoughts. You will be able to see what it is that you are doing. You will be able to see that ultimately, through recognizing your abilities to read people, you can succeed.

In this book, you will learn exactly that—you will learn the ins and outs of reading people's body language. You will learn how to tell what it is that those around you need. Little by little, you will learn about reading expressions, about how to see body language and understand other types as well. You will learn to read haptics and proxemics. You will also learn about how to use your own body language to influence other people as well. These skills matter, and the sooner that you recognize them, the better.

In particular, you will find:
- Why reading people matters and just how important it can be
- What you will need to do to read other people
- How you can begin to recognize the differences between different kinds of body language
- A guide to reading nonverbal communication
- Recognizing how to read expressions
- Learning to read the different movements of the human body, sitting, standing, open, and shut
- Recognizing how to change your own body language to utilize it
- The most common body language clusters and why they matter
- *AND MORE*

Don't let another day pass by—scroll up and click on BUY NOW today! IN doing so, you will discover that being able to read other people is easier than you thought, and you will be able to master these skills.

www.ingramcontent.com/pod-product-compliance
Lightning Source LLC
Chambersburg PA
CBHW071454070526
44578CB00001B/337